Hippopotamus

Animal
Series editor: Jonathan Burt

Already published

Albatross Graham Barwell · *Ant* Charlotte Sleigh · *Ape* John Sorenson · *Badger* Daniel Heath Justice
Bear Robert E. Bieder · *Beaver* Rachel Poliquin · *Bee* Claire Preston · *Beetle* Adam Dodd
Bison Desmond Morris · *Camel* Robert Irwin · *Cat* Katharine M. Rogers · *Chicken* Annie Potts
Cockroach Marion Copeland · *Cow* Hannah Velten · *Crocodile* Dan Wylie · *Crow* Boria Sax
Deer John Fletcher · *Dog* Susan McHugh · *Dolphin* Alan Rauch · *Donkey* Jill Bough
Duck Victoria de Rijke · *Eagle* Janine Rogers · *Eel* Richard Schweid · *Elephant* Dan Wylie
Falcon Helen Macdonald · *Flamingo* Caitlin R. Kight · *Fly* Steven Connor · *Fox* Martin Wallen
Frog Charlotte Sleigh · *Giraffe* Edgar Williams · *Goat* Joy Hinson · *Gorilla* Ted Gott and
Kathryn Weir · *Guinea Pig* Dorothy Yamamoto · *Hare* Simon Carnell · *Hedgehog* Hugh Warwick
Hippopotamus Edgar Williams · *Horse* Elaine Walker · *Hyena* Mikita Brottman · *Kangaroo* John Simons
Leech Robert G. W. Kirk and Neil Pemberton · *Leopard* Desmond Morris · *Lion* Deirdre Jackson
Llama Helen Cowie · *Lobster* Richard J. King · *Monkey* Desmond Morris · *Moose* Kevin Jackson
Mosquito Richard Jones · *Moth* Matthew Gandy · *Mouse* Georgie Carroll · *Octopus* Richard Schweid
Ostrich Edgar Williams · *Otter* Daniel Allen · *Owl* Desmond Morris · *Oyster* Rebecca Stott
Parrot Paul Carter · *Peacock* Christine E. Jackson · *Penguin* Stephen Martin · *Pig* Brett Mizelle
Pigeon Barbara Allen · *Rabbit* Victoria Dickenson · *Rat* Jonathan Burt · *Rhinoceros* Kelly Enright
Salmon Peter Coates · *Scorpion* Louise M. Pryke · *Seal* Victoria Dickenson · *Shark* Dean Crawford
Sheep Philip Armstrong · *Skunk* Alyce Miller · *Snail* Peter Williams · *Snake* Drake Stutesman
Sparrow Kim Todd · *Spider* Katarzyna and Sergiusz Michalski · *Swallow* Angela Turner
Swan Peter Young · *Tiger* Susie Green · *Tortoise* Peter Young · *Trout* James Owen
Vulture Thom van Dooren · *Walrus* John Miller and Louise Miller · *Whale* Joe Roman
Wild Boar Dorothy Yamamoto · *Wolf* Garry Marvin

Hippopotamus

Edgar Williams

REAKTION BOOKS

To Mary

Published by
REAKTION BOOKS LTD
Unit 32, Waterside
44–48 Wharf Road
London N1 7UX, UK
www.reaktionbooks.co.uk

First published 2017
Copyright © Edgar Williams 2017

Printed and bound in China

A catalogue record for this book is available from the British Library

ISBN 978 1 78023 732 9

Contents

Introduction

The hippopotamus is a uniquely African animal; it is universally recognized, with its very distinctive barrel shape and aquatic habitat. There are two species: one that is noisy and large, the common hippopotamus (*Hippopotamus amphibius*); the other – small, quiet and demure – the pygmy hippopotamus (*Choeropsis liberiensis*). The hippopotamus is the third largest land mammal after the elephant and rhinoceros. The two hippo species are the only living relatives of a long line of semiaquatic herbivorous mammals that were once found across Africa, Europe and Asia. These ancient hippos thrived, all year round, anywhere that was ice-free and warm enough to support the continuous growth of grasslands, providing them with their food.

In Earth's recent past, around 2 to 3 million years ago, the Asian climate and the tectonic orientation of the Himalayas shifted suddenly, changing the flow of drainage water more towards the south than the north, which resulted in the region's previously hospitable environment becoming more arid, driving around a dozen hippo species to extinction. The remaining ancestral species migrated into northern Europe, including modern-day Great Britain, the population thriving during the interglacial periods and dying out during each ice age. Hippo bones from these warm interglacial periods have even been found under Trafalgar Square in London. When Europe cooled after the last ice age, which

Hippopotamus, Kruger National Park, South Africa, 2004.

ended around 15,000 years ago, the hippo species that remained on the mainland – including the common hippo – perished. In the Mediterranean, some species survived on islands such as Malta. Their survival and success was thanks to their evolution into a dwarf species. A similar process occurred in Madagascar, where three dwarf hippo species survived, with one species possibly surviving until the nineteenth century.

Common hippos are communal animals that live in extended family pods, each with a dominant bull hippo protecting several females and their young. Often the pod is accompanied loosely by younger related males that the bull tolerates begrudgingly. They are adapted to an aquatic life and spend most of their day resting submerged underwater. They leave the water at dusk and feed mainly on grasses growing along the riverbank, returning in the morning to rest and ruminate. Hippos have a unique biology, such as a thick skin that serves to protect them from the fierce African midday sun as well as preventing their tissues becoming waterlogged with prolonged submersion. Hippos also have a dense bone structure, creating a skeleton that provides just the right amount of buoyancy to allow the hippo to remain effortlessly submerged. The pygmy hippo, although similar, is much smaller, and unlike its larger relative it is a solitary animal which likes to keep to itself. The jungle environment is so wet that the pygmy hippo does not need to wallow, and it often hides away in the dense jungle vegetation until dusk, when it emerges to feed on plants and roots.

In the Stone Age, the common hippo thrived, living in harmony alongside humankind; the earliest evidence of this co-existence comes in the form of the bones of butchered hippopotamuses from Ethiopia dated to 155,000 years ago. Likewise, the pygmy hippo survived in the rainforests of West Africa, serving as a source of meat for the local inhabitants.

Common hippo resting on the riverbank at sunrise.

To the ancient Egyptians, who shared the Nile river with the common hippo, it was not only hunted for its meat and the ivory from its canines, but was revered as a deity – in one form as goddess of fertility and birth, and in another form, it was associated with death. The ancient Greek scholars who travelled to Egypt provide the first description of the animals in the wild, and gave them the name 'river horse' (*hippo* meaning horse, and *potamus*, river). This primitive attempt at classification by the Greeks gave the hippo a name that has stuck ever since and is used worldwide. With the Roman conquest of Egypt, the hippopotamus was also conquered and was imported to Rome, where it was exhibited in victory celebrations, or killed in some of the many gladiatorial games. With the eventual fall of Rome came the end of Europe's association with the hippo. The only record of its existence left by the Romans was on the reverse of a few coins or in mosaics, both buried in the decay of empire.

Despite still living in the Nile river, the hippo disappears from recorded history. Then rediscovered in the fifteenth century, with

Fragment of an ancient Egyptian painting of a hippopotamus, found in Hatshepsut Hole, Deir el-Bahri, Thebes, 1922–3.

maps ever improving, the exploration of the African coast and its hinterland began. The early Portuguese explorers, followed later by merchants sailing around the Cape of Good Hope to India and beyond, soon discovered that the hippo was a common animal in southern Africa as well as in the north. Hearing of these discoveries, European scholars, especially in the Netherlands and France, called for specimens to be returned for scientific study. Hippo bones and hides were soon found in museums across Europe, and debate started as to whether the northern or southern hippo were the same or different species.

This relationship with humankind changed dramatically in 1850, when the first living hippo specimen arrived from Sudan to be studied at Regent's Park Zoological Garden in London. This single male specimen, taken from the White Nile, was a sensation not only in London, but across Europe and the USA. Overnight, everyone wanted to know everything there was to know about this strange and exotic species. This popular interest coincided with the exploration of the heartlands of Africa, where the early explorers encountered the common hippo in vast numbers. Hippos were portrayed as savage beasts capable of destroying boats and biting people in half and more ferocious than a crocodile, fulfilling the Victorian view of cruel nature being red in tooth and claw.

Then when the public thought they knew all there was to know about hippos a living specimen of a dwarf species arrived briefly in Europe. This completely new species had been identified in 1849, from a few bone and skull fragments, found tucked away deep in the West African rainforest. At first, the scientific community refused to believe it existed. This all changed when,

Mateo Hernández
(1889–1949),
hippo sculpture.

24 years later, in 1873 a live juvenile specimen finally made it to Dublin Zoo, Ireland, before promptly dying on its arrival. This hippo was not a diminutive or dwarf version of the common hippo, but a distinct new species, smaller in size, almost a living fossil, which turned out to be the closest living relative to the earlier hippos. Trying to obtain further specimens proved difficult because of the dense rainforest and wet climate of West Africa. It was only in 1912, after a heroic effort in the highland forests by a determined German explorer, Hans Schomburgk, and generous funding from Carl Hagenbeck, a wealthy animal importer, that five animals were captured and brought to Germany, and then sent on to New York. This smaller hippo was easier to keep, and it bred well in captivity, so soon most of the world's major zoos exhibited the rarer – and some might say cuter-looking – of the two species, the pygmy hippo.

Hippos have made little impact on classical art or music, and are rarely included in the portraits of animals that accompanied the Renaissance and the Enlightenment, most likely as there were no specimens mounted or alive to serve as models. The hippo has always been considered an ugly and grotesque beast, and as such has been the source of much literary inspiration, for instance being used as a metaphor for the Catholic Church by the poet T. S. Eliot. Since the twentieth century it has been commonly portrayed in children's literature and more recently in animated form in children's entertainment.

With the success of the London hippo, named Obaysch, hundreds of hippos were taken from the wild and exported to the world's zoos and circuses. The demand from the voyeuristic public has always been great. Today the hippo is found only in specialist zoos, as the enclosures needed to keep the animals in healthy conditions are complex and large. Those who are lucky enough to travel to Africa can see them in their natural habitat.

The number of hippos in Africa has shrunk, the animal first disappearing from North Africa eight millennia ago as the desertification of the Sahara spread, and then finally disappearing from the Upper Nile through excess hunting in the late nineteenth century. The hippo survives still in East, Central and South Africa, but with European colonization came the erosion of its habitat. Grazing lands were given over to cash crops and cattle, swamps were drained and rivers were dammed. Today their estimated numbers are between 125,000 and 148,000 common hippos, which is enough not to be considered endangered. Fortunately, hippo numbers are expected to increase, as they are actively managed to support a growing tourist trade. The pygmy hippo has always been rare and therefore endangered, and its numbers in the wild are estimated to be fewer than 2,500, according to the

Female pygmy hippopotamus (*Choeropsis liberiensis*), with young.

IUCN (International Union for Conservation of Nature). At the moment, its very existence is protected partly owing to a lack of interest by the locals in exploiting the forest it lives in.

Humans have grown to appreciate the hippopotamus, and to most people it is a benign, lovable creature – a mammal that seems friendly and that children find fascinating. It is a beast to be wondered at, with a long history, unique in both its biology and behaviour, surviving the ever-changing world against the odds.

1 A Tale of Two Hippos

The ancestry of the Hippopotamidae family is an interesting tale that is complicated, surprising and enigmatic. For the past two centuries palaeontologists have slowly traced their ancestry back through millions of years. Hippos belong to a particularly successful group of mammals, the order of Artiodactyls, which includes pigs, the ruminants and camels. Indeed, until recently the closest relatives to hippos were thought to be pigs and peccaries. However, as always, nature is full of surprises, and their actual closest relatives are the Cetaceans – whales, dolphins and porpoises.

Around 40 to 50 million years ago, there was a rapid expansion in the number of herbivorous mammals, particularly in the Indo-Pakistan region of Asia. This period, the Eocene, was marked by the expansion of grasslands due to an increasingly warm and wet climate. The small ancestors of Artiodactyls, the Anthracotheres, evolved rapidly into around 37 different genera and spread out across Asia, Europe and Africa, forming the suborders known today: Suidae (such as pigs), Ruminantia (such as giraffes) and Tylopoda (camels). The first hints of a distinct common ancestor of both the hippos and Cetacea – the Cetartiodactyla – can be found in the Eocene fossil record.[1] Then around 40 million years ago two sister branches rapidly appeared: the Archaeocetes and the Hippopotamidae, the latter leading to the appearance of the

Hippopotaminae in the early Miocene period (around 16–20 million years ago).

One early example is a 28-million-year-old ancestor found in Kenya, *Epirigenys lokonensis*, from *epiri*, which means 'hippo' in the Turkana language, and *Lokone*, after the site where the fossil teeth were found.[2] This distant relative is tiny in comparison to the modern common hippo, and is estimated to have weighed only around 100 kg (220 lb) – about the size of a large domestic pig. This fossil links the hippo with its forefather, the Anthracotheres (whales develop in parallel). At this time, Africa was surrounded by water, so it is a mystery how this early hippo crossed from Asia into Africa. These ancestors were the first large animals to arrive in Africa, even before giraffes and large carnivores. From this point onwards, the hippo evolved in Africa and spread across the whole continent.

The modern ancestors of the hippo finally appeared around 10 million years ago, exclusively in Africa. The sister branch

Archaepotamus harvardi, an extinct early ancestor that lived in Africa and Arabia 7.5 to 1.8 million years ago.

evolved rapidly, transforming from terrestrial mammals to marine mammals in a relatively short period of time, losing their limbs and becoming the Cetacea of today – whales, dolphins and porpoises. The Hippopotaminae continued to evolve until around 7 to 8 million years ago, when the first large animals appeared. This is known as the 'hippotamine event', when the fossil record suddenly becomes very abundant.[3] This increase in abundance is again thought to coincide with newly plentiful grasslands and an ample supply of herbaceous material to eat.

Today's hippos are represented by two living monotypic genera, *Hippopotamus* and *Choeropsis*. In the past, the genus *Hexaprotodonta* contained more than thirty named fossil species – such as hippopothamus, hippotamus and hyppopotamus – and was found across Europe, Asia and Africa.[4]

The Asian hippopotamids were more closely related to the modern pygmy hippo than to the common hippo and thus carry the genus name *Hexaprotodon* (the connection between *Hexaprotodon* and the pygmy hippo has been made through the dentition, as many of the early fossils are identified through the remains of

Anthracotherium magnum, a hippo ancestor.

17

jaw bones and teeth).[5] The earliest specimens of *Hexaprotodon* or *Choeropsis* are from Kenya and date from 8 million years ago; the present pygmy hippo, a living fossil, is more similar to these earlier ancestors than the common hippo.[6] In Asia, from 6 to 3 million years ago, around eleven distinct hexaprotodon species existed.[7] The remains of one, *Hexaprotodon sivalensis,* has been found in Pakistan, northern and central India, Myanmar, southwestern China, Sri Lanka, western Thailand, Malaysia and Java. This migrant species from Africa was successful in populating this region because the climate was wet and warm, with plenty of grassy floodplains offering an abundance of food. Then, by around 2 to 3 million years ago, the hexaprotodon species all but disappeared from Asia – this vanishing coincided with a change in the climate, and the last period of glaciation. The altered climate intensified the monsoons, which were particularly challenging for a large semiaquatic species like the hippo because prolonged, dry winter monsoons led to longer droughts, and eventually the retreat of the grassy floodplains, creating a shortage of food and habitat. Further, a tectonic-induced shift in the orientation of the Himalayas altered river drainage and reduced the floodplains even more. These factors were severe enough to reduce the population again until finally driving the Asian pygmy hippos to extinction.[8] The other African animals, such as the elephant or rhinoceros, were not affected so severely and adapted to the new climate, surviving today as the Asian elephant, and the Javan and Indian rhinos. The Asian ancestor of the giraffe was also affected by the change in vegetation and became extinct at the same time. In the Arabian peninsula, the remaining hexaprotodon species clung on a bit longer but finally disappeared about 1 million years ago.

Some of the early European explorers mistakenly took these Asian fossil hippo remains as evidence that the hippo still lived in the Indus valley region and Java, a view supported by historical tales such as the one given by Alexander the Great, who was purported to have come across hippos in India, such as the one given by the Greek historian Onesicritus (360–290 BC) who accompanied Alexander the Great on his Asian campaigns. Onesicritus, when comparing the Nile and Indus, stated that both rivers contain crocodiles and hippopotamuses. He was probably mistaken about the Indus and has since been criticized for being inaccurate. In fact, it was thought that the early hippo had existed all over the world. In the late nineteenth century some biologists discovered hippo teeth in several locations around Cuba, and suggested that hippos once occupied the island. The teeth were, in fact, from recent hippopotamuses and were actually discarded teeth which had been used by dentists as false teeth and had been thrown away following the introduction of the more popular porcelain false teeth.[9] Similarly, what was thought to be a hippo tooth unearthed in Trimble County, Kentucky, turned out to be a mastodon tooth.[10] In China, a supposed hippo find turned out to be

Hexaprotodon sivalensis, an early ancestor with charactersitics of both the modern common and pygmy hippopotamus. It lived in the Indian subcontinent about 6 million years ago.

from a rhinoceros, whereas a presumed hippo radius bone found in Australia was not from a hippo but from an ape.[11]

In Europe, hippopotamus species (*Hippopotamus amphibius*, *H. gorgops* and *H. antiquus*) survived, as the climate remained sufficiently warm to support indigenous hippos, and further migrant African species were able to populate the region as well. They spread out across the Mediterranean lands from Greece to Spain and up into northern Europe, even colonizing the British Isles before the English Channel formed.

Two species of hippos colonized Britain: the common hippopotamus and *Hippopotamus major*. This colonization took place on two separate occasions during interglacial periods: first, around half a million years ago, during the Cromerian stage, and second during the Eemian interglacial (sometimes called the Ipswichian interglacial) period, around 115,000–130,000 years ago.[12] This last colonization was particularly successful, and skeletal and tooth remains of the common hippopotamus have been found as far north as Stockton-on-Tees, in North and South Wales and in southern England from Devon to Kent, along the Severn and Thames rivers. Most remains have been found in alluvial beds deposited alongside rivers. Such gravel deposits explain the hippo remains found under Trafalgar Square in central London in 1957.[13] The plant remains associated with these bones suggested that the climate was similar to the climate in central France today. Similar hippo finds were recovered from around the river Rhine in northern Germany and the Netherlands.[14]

The hippo fragments are often found along with other large mammals like oxen, rhino and mammoths. These animals were able to survive in both warm and cold climates, adapting to cold climates by growing long, woolly coats as the woolly rhino and mammoth did; this was not an option for the hairless hippo, and it could not survive cold winters. This is supported by the fact that although the hippo was found alongside the remains of these woolly animals, it has never been found next to truly cold-climate-adapted animals such as reindeer. Thus as a consequence of climate change, and though they outlived their Asian relatives, the remaining hippopotamus species could not ultimately survive in northern or central Europe, as the winter temperatures were too cold. Their last refuge was southern Italy, where they finally disappeared around 100,000 years ago.[15]

While Europe underwent cycles of glaciation, the African continent enjoyed a period of high rainfall which subsequently increased the aquatic habitats for the hippo. It was during this period that the hippo species were able to spread homogenously across the continent, thus providing an explanation for why the modern hippos share similar genotypes, despite these populations being geographically isolated today.[16]

The first recorded hippopotamus remains of extant and extinct species were found around 1800 in Walton and Brentford, London, and bones, teeth and tusks have been found regularly in England's southern regions ever since – anywhere gravel extraction occurs.[17] Today these finds rarely make the headlines, but in the nineteenth century they were considered sensational news items, and in some cases they became museum centre-pieces, such as the Barrington Hippo in 1879, now on display at the Sedgwick Museum of Earth Sciences at the University of Cambridge, and the Allenton Hippo unearthed in 1895, now on display at the Derby Museum and Art Gallery. The hippopotamus was even implicated in the great Piltdown Man hoax of 1912, when Charles Dawson, an amateur archaeologist and geologist, claimed to have found two human skulls from unknown primitive hominids in Piltdown Quarry, East Sussex; the finds were described as the missing links between apes and man. This discovery was sensational and reported around the world. Surrounding these early human bones were remnants from other fossil animals, including a hippopotamus tooth. The hoax was not uncovered until 1953, when the skulls were re-examined and found to be medieval in origin, with the jaw of an orangutan added. While the tooth was not from the common hippo, it was still genuine and from an extinct dwarf species. Its origin was probably Malta or Sicily. Dawson had spent two months touring the Mediterranean on his honeymoon in 1907, and around this time fossilized dwarf hippos were discovered in limestone caves in Malta. The find was widely publicized in the Maltese press, but if and how Doyle obtained a tooth while in Malta is not known.

As mainland Europe cooled during the Eemian interglacial period, some species became stranded on what are today the Mediterranean islands; during the ice ages, these islands were mountainous regions surrounded by dry land, as the level of the Mediterranean Sea was much lower then. These isolated hippos thrived as an island species. Biology dictates that for a large species to survive on an island, it must, over time, decrease in size and become a dwarf species, a process of endemism known as island dwarfism. While the geographical isolation offers some advantages such as protection from predators, its disadvantages become apparent as the population expands and food supply becomes a limiting factor. Thus for a breeding population of hippopotamuses to survive with good genetic diversity, evolution tends to drive the body mass down. These dwarf species are actually miniature versions, unlike the modern pygmy hippo which is a true pygmy species (a pygmy is not a reduced version and is naturally small, whereas a dwarf species is a scaled-down, or diminutive, version of the original normal-sized hippo) and is, in some ways – by living in isolated pockets of wet jungle – an island species.

From the Miocene, dwarf hippos lived on several Mediterranean islands, the smallest (*Phanourios minor*) being found on

Cyprus, and the largest (*Hippopotamus pentlandi*) on Sicily; other species where found on Crete (*Hippopotamus creutzburgi*) and Malta (*Hippopotamus melitensis*). These species had different feet and dentition, representing adaptations to specialist diets and terrestrial habitats, and they grazed on grassy hillsides rather than on the flat, grassy floodplains which their African cousins inhabited. It was thought that these hippos coexisted alongside man, and were hunted to extinction by them, but it now seems that the hippos died out from a series of long droughts before there was any permanent habitation by man.[18]

Dwarf hippos endemic to islands have also been found in Madagascar in the Indian Ocean and in Java (*Hexaprotodon sivajavanicus*).[19] In Madagascar, the semi-fossilized remains of three separate dwarf species have been found. These now-extinct species occupied different areas of the island. *Hippopotamus madagascariensis* lived in the central highlands and northwest; *Hippopotamus lemerlei* lived only in the southwestern lowlands facing continental Africa; and *Hippopotamus laloumena* lived solely on the east coast. The remains date to around 10,000 years ago, during the Holocene epoch. It seems likely that two of these species were still thriving two millennia ago, when the first humans arrived and colonized the island. It is hard to gauge when exactly they became extinct, but there were sightings recorded when the Europeans arrived in the sixteenth century. The French governor of Madagascar, Étienne de Flacourt, published a description of the native fauna in his *Histoire de la grande isle Madagascar* (1661). One of the unidentified animals in his book is the *mangarsahoc*.[20] While the description is vague and it is a second-hand rendering, the illustration looks like a pygmy hippo. Later, a French geographer and ethnologist, Alfred Grandidier, while on an expedition to the island interior in 1868, heard native Malagasy accounts of a strange beast they called *song'aomby*, which translates as 'cow

that isn't a cow'. One day, while making further enquiries about these creatures, a village chieftain took Grandidier to a local marsh and indicated that it was full of *song'aomby* bones. Excited, Alfred stripped off, jumped into the marsh and immediately discovered several large bones, of which some were of the elephant bird. This was exciting in itself, as these were some of the first elephant bird bones, or remains of the mythical roc, to be found, but his luck continued: he also found some hippo bones.[21] He named the unknown hippo species *Hippopotamus lemerlei* in honour of his odd-job man, Lemerl, from home in France.[22] Unsubstantiated sightings of pygmy hippos continued until the twentieth century, and some biologists believe they still survive today in some remote corner of Madagascar.[23]

The three species are thought to have arrived on the island at separate times, and all originated from *Hippopotamus amphibius.* Thus their lineage does not date back to when Madagascar was part of the supercontinent Gondwana (180–300 million years ago), but to when separated from the African mainland by 425 km (264 miles) of the Indian Ocean.

How these animals reached the island is a mystery that is still hotly debated today.[24] To establish a successful breeding colony would require at the very minimum a male and a female hippo. Ideally, several pairs are needed to produce a strong genetic stock and healthy gene pool. There are not many options for crossing such a large expanse of ocean – one possibility would be via a land bridge (long gone, due to erosion or covered by rising sea levels), while another option would be if the hippos rafted or swam over.

The latter explanation is still disputed by scientists, as mass colonization by rafting on floating vegetation or swimming seems improbable. While rafting on mats of floating vegetation seems plausible for a small animal, for hippos it is highly unlikely. Swimming is the favoured route by other scientists. However, hippos are not able to swim long distances, and although in modern times hippos have been seen close to the shore, none have been seen swimming any considerable distance from the shore or found at sea. Most zoologists argue that the hippos' physiology makes them too heavy to swim. When in deep water, hippos walk and hop along the river bottom while holding their breath. If the water is too deep, they might drown, as they are unable to surface for air. Thus travelling across the sea in this way seems highly improbable. There is some evidence that a land bridge, or an island chain, once linked Africa and Madagascar during the Eocene; this may have coincided with a sea level low enough in places for the hippos eventually to migrate to the island.[25] The fact that hippos arrived on the island on at least three occasions is indisputable, but the theories of how they appeared are mere speculation and it remains one of the biggest mysteries in biology.

Millions of years ago, the early hippopotamuses and whales shared a common terrestrial ancestor. Looking at the biology and behaviour of the two remaining hippo species, we see some common features with the Cetaceans: both hippos and Cetaceans require an aqueous environment for survival, and many of their physiological adaptations for aquatic living have parallels in whales and dolphins.

Despite being widespread throughout Europe, Asia and Africa, the hippopotamus slowly succumbed to adverse climate change, as the uppermost northern limits for its survival moved ever southwards until its only habitat was the African continent. Here it thrived until modern times. The pygmy hippo, originally including many parallel species, was the ultimate survivor and remained largely hidden until its discovery by Europeans in the nineteenth century. The history of the modern hippo parallels that of two other ancestral cousins and members of the even-toed ungulates: the giraffe and okapi. One is a common species found across Africa, and the other, the okapi, is a rare jungle-bound species that lives in West Africa that was discovered in the early twentieth century.

The long evolution of these two semiaquatic mammals, the common hippo and the pygmy hippo, with their relationship to whales, gives them a unique heritage among terrestrial mammals.

Two pygmy hippos in a 20th-century illustration.

The consequences are a biology and behaviour perfectly adapted for survival in an ecological niche only occupied by fish and reptiles. Hippotamidae's love of water is one thing everybody recognizes and has many advantages as well as disadvantages, as a close look at their biology and behaviour will show.

2 Mud, Mud, Glorious Mud

Common hippos are semiaquatic animals that like to spend their days largely submerged in water, mainly in rivers and lakes with gently sloping banks, often sharing their habitat with crocodiles. The common hippo is a gregarious species that likes to congregate in family groups, consisting of a dominant male, several females and a number of youngsters. At night, they leave the water and journey inland to feed on grass and vegetation, consuming prodigious amounts. To follow this daily regime requires a specialized biology that is only found in the hippo. The pygmy hippo has a similar biology, but behaves differently and prefers a solitary existence in its hot, dank and humid jungle environment.

The name hippopotamus is compounded from two Greek nouns: *hippos* (horse) and *potamus* (river). The ancient Greek scholars, such as Herodotus in 440 BC, promoted this name, based on the view that the submerged head, with its eyes, ears and snout showing above the water, looks horse-like. Its dung smells like horse dung, and to some, its snorts sound like a horse. We now know that 'hippopotamus' is a misnomer, and the hippo is not related to the horse nor does not it look like one when out of the water. If the animal were discovered today, it would be hard to ascribe it a name. It was Carl Linnaeus (1707–1778), the Swedish botanist and taxonomist, who, in 1758, gave the common hippopotamus its full name, *Hippopotamus amphibius*, in recognition of

its semi-amphibious nature and not its amphibious lineage. There is only one species, but some sources identify three subspecies: *Hippopotamus amphibius amphibius*, *Hippopotamus amphibius capensis* (the South African hippo) and *Hippopotamus amphibious kiboko* from Kenya and Somalia, *kiboko* being the Swahili name for hippopotamus.[1]

A group of hippopotamuses drinking and resting in the river and on the shore. Colour lithograph after W. Kuhnert, 1916.

The Latin plural for 'hippopotamus' is 'hippopotami', and this form was in vogue during the mid-nineteenth century; its use has since declined and is now only used in scientific publications. An equally valid plural is 'hippopotamuses', which became increasingly popular until the beginning of the twentieth century. After this, its popularity waned, and the shortened form 'hippos' became the more commonly used plural and is today the most accepted form. Edward Lear (1812–1888), the English artist, illustrator, musician, author and poet, suggested humorously that a better name for a hippo would be 'hippopotamouse' – this would make the plural hippopotamice.[2]

The pygmy hippo (*Hexaprotodon liberiensis*) was not known to the ancients, and there is no written trace or any ancient reference to its existence, despite the fact that Europeans visited the west coast of Africa from the fifteenth century onwards. It was not until 1844 that the pygmy hippo was first described scientifically by the American physician and natural scientist Dr Samuel George Morton (1799–1851), based on analysis of bone and skull fragments returned to Britain.[3] Dr Morton first named it *Hippopotamus minor*, but this name had already been used for a fossil hippo discovered previously, so in 1849 he changed it to *Hippopotamus liberiensis* and then again, finally ending up with *Choeropsis liberiensis*. *Choeropsis* resembles the Greek *khoiros*, a pig or hog, with *opsis* meaning 'belonging to'. The *liberiensis* refers to its West African habitat on the coast in modern-day Liberia. The common name was the 'little' or 'Liberian hippopotamus'.[4] In 1977 its Latin name was changed again, this time to *Hexaprodenta liberiensis*.[5] The name change was made in recognition of its ancestral link to previously discovered extinct Asian species which had three pairs of incisors or 'six front teeth', hence the name *Hexa* ('six') *prodonta* ('front teeth'). Oddly, the modern pygmy hippo has only a single pair of front teeth, so it should be called *diprodonta*. Today the pygmy hippo population is confined to Sierra Leone, Liberia, Guinea and the Ivory Coast in West Africa. A separate population was once thought to exist in the Niger delta and was considered a subspecies called *Hexaprodonta liberiensis heslopi*. The continued existence of the Niger pygmy hippopotamus is now in doubt, as there have been no reported sightings for more than fifty years.

The common and pygmy hippo species do not overlap geographically, except for a small area where the common hippo occupies the large rivers such as the Niger. The pygmy hippo prefers the border zones between rainforest and swamps. Because of its damp and dark rainforest environment, its skin is kept moist and is not exposed to direct sunlight; thus it does not need to spend all day immersed underwater, preferring to stay in shade instead.[6]

The pygmy hippo is a solitary animal; the females prefer to live in their own territories and actively avoid other females and males. They rely on smell, marking their territory with dung; they have acute hearing, as sight is not very effective in dense vegetation. Males are more aggressive and so are solitary by mutual consent; they tend to have larger territories than females, and a male territory may encompass the territories of several females. This behaviour serves to maintain adequate food supply but also allows sufficient contact between animals to ensure a healthy, diverse breeding population. With estimated numbers being around 2,000 to 3,000, the pygmy hippo is rare.

Hippo, with scars visible on its side, stands beside the water with two oxpeckers perched on its back.

Alert hippopotamus, Maasai Mara, Kenya, 2007.

Young hippos playing in the water, Maasai Mara, Kenya, 2007.

In contrast, the common hippopotamus is found across continental Africa south of the Sahara Desert and is one of the world's largest terrestrial animals, only outweighed by elephants and rhinoceroses. A male at 3–5 m (10–17 ft) in length can weigh up to 3.5 tonnes; a female is lighter, up only to 2.3 tonnes, and shorter at 3–4 m (10–14 ft). Beyond their size, there is little to tell the sexes apart, especially when young. The most recognizable feature, however, is not their size but their shape: they have barrel-like

Hippos sparring.

trunks, covered in hairless skin with a brownish-pink tinge. At each corner, they have thick, stumpy legs, each foot having four short, conical toes connected by small webs. A pad of solid tissue on the heel provides support. The feet are well adapted for walking in wet, slippery mud and soft earth. The same overall appearance is true of the pygmy hippo.

The rear end has a short, stumpy, hairless and bristle-tipped tail. These bristles are similar to those found in seals and sea lions, providing another connection to aquatic animals.[7] The tail plays an important role in marking a male hippo's, or bull's, territory. The tail is rotated rapidly when the animal defecates, ensuring that its semi-liquid dung mixed with urine is spread over as wide an area as possible. The bulls mark their territories in this way, even spraying their fellow cows (females) and juveniles. Once sprayed, a cow will urinate, and this submissive behaviour allows the bull to sample the urine and assess her reproductive status. When another male enters his territory, the two bulls both spray dung around as a warning. If this stand-off does not work, the two

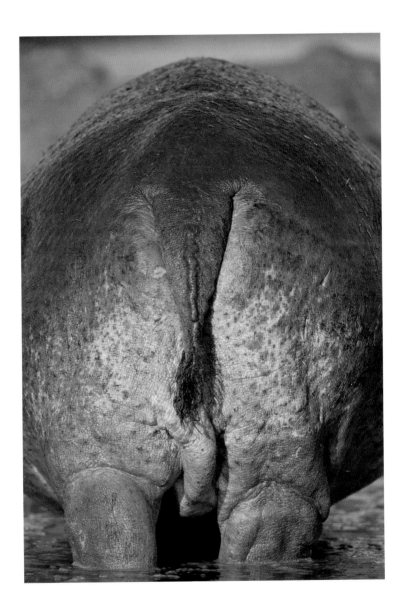

bulls will fight one another, usually in the water in front of the rest of the herd. This is when hippos are at their noisiest, as the herd and the fighting animals growl at each other. The fights can continue until one of the bulls is killed. The two bulls attack each other with their huge mouths. Pygmy hippos also like to spray dung with their tails, using it to mark their territories.

A hippo's head in proportion to its body is huge. The head is as an 'hourglass' shape, being wide across the eyeline, with ears high on the head, and then narrowing before widening again to a fleshy snout, with two prominent nostrils on top. The eyes work well both in water and in air and are placed high, so that they can act periscopically when the animal is submerged. The alignment of the eyes, ears and nostrils allows them all to break the surface of the water together. Thus, when the water is still, all that shows of the hippo is its eyes, ears and nostrils. The hippo skull is large compared to the rest of the animal, while the skull

The short bristled tail of the common hippopotamus.

Hippopotamus showing yawning behaviour, Garamba National Park, Democratic Republic of the Congo, 1991.

Adult hippopotamus showing the red colouration of the skin around the muzzle and eyes, South Luangwa National Park, Zambia, 2010s.

space enclosing the brain is proportionate for its size – it is the bony skull base and jaw bones that are bulky. In relation to its size the hippo has the fifth-heaviest brain among mammals, after the elephant, human, camel and giraffe: weighing around 580 g (20 oz), the hippo has a brain-to-body-weight ratio of 1:2,789, compared to our human ratio of 1:40. The forehead of the pygmy hippo is convex in shape instead of concave, and its eyes are not elevated. While the common hippo can see, hear and sniff without revealing itself above water, the pygmy is not adapted for living underwater.

In the common hippo, the lower jaw is hinged at the back of the skull in such a way that the hippo can lock its mouth wide open, almost to 180°. This so-called 'yawning' action is important during combat with other hippos and when tackling crocodiles. The skull's mid-section, which gives it the hourglass shape, accommodates the cheek teeth for grinding. The front section holds the incisors and canines. Two large, curved canines or tusks project outside the front corners of the lower jaw and point vertically. The constantly growing tusks look like small elephant tusks. The two incisors between the canines point forward and are smaller and less curved. The straight tusks are specifically structured to function for piercing, that is, fighting, while the curved incisors are adapted for levering (for example, roots, as they eat herbaceous plants) and to resist bending. The upper jaw has a similar arrangement, except the teeth are smaller, and the canines project downwards. The lower and upper canines, or tusks, oppose one another and rub against each other, which leads to the tips becoming sharp, making them more lethal when fighting. The surface of hippo tusks is different from the ivory of other animals, as instead of just consisting of dentine (the white organic material inside teeth) the tusks are covered in an additional layer of hard enamel (the outer covering of teeth), making hippo ivory more durable

Submerged hippo showing the aligned placement of eyes, ears and nose, Garamba National Park, Democratic Republic of the Congo, 1991.

than elephant ivory.[8] The arrangement of the front canines and incisors, and the generous, bristly lips, allow the mouth to be closed tightly, making it waterproof when submerged. The common hippo has 36 teeth, and the pygmy hippo 34.[9] The back molars are for feeding, and in both species there are six in each jaw – three premolars and three molars.

The jaw has to be powerful in order to be able to use these teeth as weapons, so the large lower jaw is endowed with extra-large muscles; these muscles give the hippo its extra jowls, making it look as if it is always smiling. The jaw also generates a huge bite pressure of more than 126 kgf/cm^2 (kilograms per square centimetre) or 1,800 PSI (pounds per square inch). Although less than the massive 420 kgf/cm^2 (6,000 psi) of the Nile crocodile (*Crocodylus niloticus*), this is still formidable enough pressure to break bones and snap wooden boats in two.[10]

While the jaws are powerful and the canines inflict serious wounds and root up aquatic plants, they are of no use when eating vegetable matter. Like other large herbivores, the hippo eats using its tough lips to grasp and crop the grass; this – combined with rear, flat molars for grinding up the fodder – allows them to create a coarse mash. The mash is then moved to the back of the mouth using the tongue and swallowed by raising the head.

Hippopotamuses are vocal animals, and people living near the common hippopotamus often comment on their noisy calls. They use two forms of communication: vocally in the air – when out of the water or with their heads raised out of the water – and subsonically when submerged under the water. They can do both at the same time if their mouths are only partially submerged. Both genders can generate loud calls that can carry for several kilometres. The normal hippo voice is the bellow, which is called honking but sounds like a deep tonal laugh.[11] They also roar, which sounds like a cross between a lion and an elephant, and

38

often the early African explorers mistook hippos for lions as they sat around their campfires at night. Female hippos roar at each other if they are stressed or annoyed by a bull. Vocal communication is used in spreading an alert of an approaching predator such as a lion or humans. The sound also serves to deter lions from coming any closer.[12] A male calling from one pod will often imitate a call from a male in a nearby pod and so on; a call can thereby travel along the river very quickly, covering several kilometres in a few minutes.

Amphibious underwater communication is more subtle and outside our audible range. It is extremely important, as it allows communication between submerged herd members and individual hippos, such as between a mother and her calf. Because hippos live in muddy and opaque water, sight is not much use, so they can use the sound to locate each other. These noises are described as grunts, croaks, whines, screams and clicks. They are made while the animal holds its breath – the noises are generated in the throat, without opening the mouth and nostrils and therefore without expelling air. The transmitted sound vibrations do not travel down the outer ear, as this is closed when underwater; instead, the vibrations are funnelled to the inner ear by transmission along the jaw bone and skull, a process that involves the

Hippos in a water hole, Okavango Delta, Botswana.

petrosal bone.[13] This is very similar to the way sound is perceived by hippos' distant cousins, the dolphins and whales.

A recent scientific study of the hippo's acoustic repertoires was conducted on captive hippos kept in Disney's Animal Kingdom, in Orlando, Florida. The team from Manhattan College in New York found that 80 per cent of the communication took place underwater, and they identified eleven different vocalizations, with snorts, grunts and growls associated with dominant behaviour, and chuffs, groans and whines with submissive behaviour.[14]

The common hippo has taken full advantage of an aquatic lifestyle, and is unique among large terrestrial animals in spending a significant proportion of its life either completely submerged in water or at least wallowing in muddy pools. While this aquatic adaptation might reflect its common origins with cetaceans and limit its distribution to major waterways, it provides the hippo

The ears and eyes of the common hippo are small relative to its size.

with several unique advantages. The water provides support and gives the hippo much greater mobility. The buoyancy of the hippo is balanced in such a way as to keep the hippo largely submerged – it has a greater body density compared to other large terrestrial mammals.[15] This is the result of more compact bones, a natural process known as osteosclerosis in which the bones grow with thicker walls.[16]

This heavier density means, as mentioned earlier, that submerged hippos cannot – or at least, do not – swim; they always walk, or when in deeper water they gallop or leap, porpoising, or hopping, along the bottom.[17] This bottom-walking ability is only found in a few other animals such as the nine-banded armadillo (*Dasypus novemcinctus*), although the armadillo is only capable of doing it in shallow water. It is thought that the early ancestors of the hippo developed this bounce.

Immersion helps maintain body temperature, the surrounding water cooling the body down during the daytime, when the air temperature is at its fiercest and most large African mammals seek shade or at least become inactive. The hippo, which cannot sweat, has to keep cool by submerging itself in water. Maintaining body temperature enables the hippo to survive with a slower metabolic rate and therefore a reduced need for calories and food. When submerged, its heart rate slows from sixty to twenty beats per minute, and when immersed with its nostrils above the surface, it breathes slowly, at around seven to ten breaths per minute. After diving, an adult often holds its breath for about five minutes before resurfacing for another intake of air, its nostrils just breaking the top of the water. The nostrils are situated high on the front of the upper jaw and will be the first structure to break water when the hippo lifts its head. When threatened, a hippo has been known to hold its breath for thirty minutes, while young hippos have been known to last twenty minutes. The hippo will shut its nose and ears automatically upon contact with water – the openings are ringed by sphincter muscles. The ears are quite mobile and nimble when flicking off flies; when the hippo is submerged, the ears are tucked backwards. The ability to hold their breath and to make their airways watertight allows calves to suckle underwater.[18] Hippos, when fully immersed, can see underwater because their eyes are equipped with a special clear, protective membrane.

Thanks to their aqueous lifestyle, hippos never become dehydrated while they have sufficient water to wallow in, which keeps them from having to trek large distances to a watering hole for a drink each day.

All large mammals suffer from external parasites, which, in African mammals, are removed by birds. This is also true for the hippo, but by being submerged, it can also be serviced by fish. Several species of fish have been observed cleaning hippos – one species, a cichlid, removes material from just around the tails and rear, while another species cleans the cracks and crevices of the feet. Another species cleans or picks at the wounds, which is not always an advantage, as it can prevent wound-healing. Carp also benefit from the algae that thrive in nutrient-rich water created by hippo waste.[19]

Living in the water provides protection from predators such as lions, especially for the younger hippos. Hippos do share the water with crocodiles, but most of the time each species shows a healthy respect for the other's privacy, and their paths rarely cross. Hippos do not seem to be afraid of crocodiles and have been known to protect other animals such as antelope from being ambushed by submerged crocodiles.[20] A bull hippo is quite capable of killing a crocodile, either by trampling or biting.

Reliance on submergence in water has a downside in that hippos cannot live in regions which experience long arid periods or dry

The skin's red colouring is most prominent around the neck and head, the areas exposed to the sun above the water.

seasons, nor where the ambient water temperature drops below 15°C (59°F) or undergoes periods of freezing. Sensitivity to the ambient temperature is reflected in hippo behaviour: on cool and windy days, hippos will stay in the water longer than usual, and if the water is cold, in the mornings they will bask in the sun to warm themselves up. Their large size, and barrelled body shape, serves to reduce the ratio of their surface area to their overall mass, making it easier to maintain a constant body temperature of 35.4°C (95.7°F).[21]

Another reason the hippo relies on submergence is that its skin is remarkably sensitive to the drying effect of the hot sun. Hippo skin is thick and largely hairless, similar to elephant and rhinoceros skin – so-called pachydermous skin. At its thickest around its back, it can be up to 3.5 cm (1½ in.) thick, which, when dried, can be used to make good-quality leather. It is thinnest around its belly, at 1 cm (0.4 in.) thick. Below the skin is a layer of fat, weighing in total around 90 kg (200 lb).[22] In a hot climate, this fat can be drained from the carcass as an oil – what the Afrikaners call *spek* – and can be preserved by mixing it with salt. The fat/oil is very similar to whale oil, again a shared characteristic with Cetaceans.[23]

The skin has some unusual properties: it is tough but 'leaky', so it loses water quickly in the sunshine. Hippos have no sweat glands, and they are very sensitive to ultraviolet rays and hence sunburn. The skin colour is homogenous, ranging from grey to black, and seems to glisten as if it is wet. This sheen is due to secretions of a sticky goo from subdermal glands. The rate of secretion can vary widely and increases with stress. The secretion makes the skin slippery to the touch. This alkaline exudate is initially colourless, but when exposed to light, it quickly turns a reddish-pink colour. This observation has led to the legend that

Secretion-free hippopotamus skin, which is brown to grey in colour, with only a hint of pink.

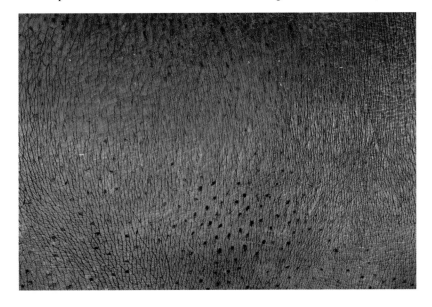

hippos sweat blood. A team of Japanese chemists in 2004 found that the exudate contains two pigments: a red one, called hipposudoric acid, and an orange pigment named norhipposudoric acid.[24] This extraordinary exudate not only moistens the skin but, more importantly, acts like a sunscreen and filters out harmful ultraviolet light. When the skin dries in the air, the exudate dries to a brown-coloured lacquer which serves to protect the skin from desiccation. The exudate also has antiseptic properties, which help when the skin is broken, especially useful when living in such a muddy environment. It is secreted mostly during the day, even underwater, reflecting its role in thermoregulation. Its secretion during stress and exertion is similar to other animals' propensity to sweat under emotional conditions.[25] The skin of the pygmy hippo, though similar to that of the common hippo – at around 1 cm (0.4 in.) thick – is black in colour; it secretes the same pink exudate, as well as a white foamy secretion when the hippo exerts itself.[26]

After spending most of the daylight hours in the water, hippos leave to feed on land at dusk or sunset, grazing on the adjacent riverbanks when grass is plentiful. They will, however, travel 2–3 km (1–2 miles) during drier times to find green pastures. If there are humans around, they may wait until darkness falls before they leave their safe, aquatic havens. Hippos will take advantage of a moonless night to leave early for grazing. When travelling overland, they follow the same route each night, to and fro, eventually creating a well-worn path. Hippos are not communal grazers and spread out once they reach their grazing grounds. They are so efficient at grazing that soon so-called hippo lawns – that is, lawns created by close-cropping of the grass every night – are created. Hippos will feed on waterborne vegetation as well. After around five hours of feeding, the hippos return to the water. The rutted trails interspersed with dung heaps are easy to follow in the dark,

Hippopotamus from A. B. Strong's 19th-century *Illustrated Natural History of the Three Kingdoms*.

and once back in the water the hippos relax to digest their food, socialize with one another and sleep. Unlike other ruminants, the hippo does not regurgitate its food for a second chew; instead, the forage ferments in the stomach, and it takes several hours before any nutrition is extracted from the food. Digestion continues in the long intestines.[27] The hippo therefore needs to eat huge quantities of food to get the nutrients it needs, around 40 kg (88 lb) each day. This is less than a ruminant of similar size, but because the hippo lazes around in the water, burning fewer calories, it survives.

Although they are predominantly grazers, if given the opportunity to intrude onto cultivated land, hippos will consume maize, sugar cane, pumpkins, beans, cabbages and melons. Hippos have been known to exhibit carnivory as well, having been observed eating the carcasses of other animals – mainly antelope killed by

Hippo footprint showing the circular-shaped foot and four forward-facing toes.

animals such as crocodiles or hunting dogs.[28] Cannibalism of recently dead and decaying carcasses has also been noted and reported several times. Both carnivory and cannibalism are thought to occur when food is in short supply during the dry season. This behaviour also leads to the spread among hippos of fatal diseases, such as anthrax.[29]

Lone hippo on its way to feeding grounds.

Hippos have positive effects on the local ecosystems. The nightly grazing keeps the pasture clear of woody plant species, which benefits other grazing animals such as the kob antelope (*Kobus kob*). The fresh grass shoots that spring up after the grazing hippo has passed on are also more nutritious.[30] Moreover, the prodigious amount of dung produced by hippos can heavily fertilize the local waterways, having a positive impact on the fish population.[31]

Another ecological benefit of the hippo is their regular movement to their feeding grounds, which leads to the development of channels free of vegetation and allows the expansion of waterways.

When water levels increase after rain, these channels can become permanently flooded.[32] However, it is a delicate balance, and if there are too many hippos (more than $31/km^2$, or over 81 per $mile^2$), overgrazing can be devastating and cause extreme soil erosion.[33] Hippos living near human settlements have always been a problem, as they have no respect for crops: a hippo can destroy a field of crops in one night, either by eating most of the plants or by trampling those that are uneaten.

It is only at night, or at dawn or dusk, when the hippos migrate away from their basking to their feeding areas, that their agility can be appreciated. Hippos can reach speeds of up to 30 kph (19 mph) and are quite unstoppable if charging. When walking on land, they always have three feet on the ground, giving them plenty of support and allowing them to trot when running.[34] Thus, while it is fairly easy to paddle out of the way of an immersed hippo, on land it is not so easy to outrun – hiding behind a tree or, even better, climbing a tree is a better way to avoid being trampled or bitten.

The pygmy hippo has an altogether different diet, since it lives in lush forest, where it can crop grasses using its lips and eat saplings, bushes, herbs, ferns, fallen fruit and aquatic vegetation. Unlike the common hippo, it use its canines to tear up plant material. It has a similar digestive system. Feeding can occur all the time, as the jungle environment is humid and warm.

Breeding in the common hippo begins in the dry season between May and July, so births occur in the wet season, January to March, when food is plentiful and supports lactation. The gestation period is around 32 to 37 weeks, and usually one calf is born, although twins occur in around 1 in 280 births.[35] This is a relatively short gestation time, especially for such a large animal. The bulls reach sexual maturity after four to eleven years; for the females, it is around seven to fifteen years. Hippos in the wild have a lifespan of forty to fifty years, females on average living longer than males. A young bull usually finds its first mate from the herd it has grown up with, or at least one nearby. The bull does so by cautiously approaching a female in oestrous. A receptive female gestures submission by crouching and defecating. Once the bull finds a receptive cow, he will chase her into shallow water and mate with her, while making a loud, honking noise. This occurs in the water, which helps to support the weight of the bull. Usually,

all that can be seen of the female is her head appearing occasionally above water to draw breath.

As the birth approaches, the cow becomes ever more aggressive. A few weeks before the birth, she leaves the herd. Finally, just before the birth, she finds shallow water such as a reed bed, or may even venture onto the bank. At birth, the calf weighs anything from 35 to 55 kg (77 to 120 lb), and is about 90 cm long (about 3 ft). Newborn calves can walk within minutes of being born and are equally at home in water. The young hippo can close its mouth and hold its breath when underwater. It can only hold its breath for a short period underwater, however, so the mother must support the calf by holding it up with her snout in order for it to take breaths above the surface. The ability to hold its breath allows the young hippo to feed while underwater. The calf feeds from two teats between the mother's rear legs.

The mother aggressively defends her young from predators such as crocodiles, lions and hyenas, but also from male hippos. This dependency ensures that the young hippo imprints on its mother. Orphan hippo calves have been known to imprint on

Hippopotamuses
moving through
a canal made by
frequent use, in a
freshwater marsh,
Okavango Delta,
Moremi Game
Reserve, Botswana,
2014.

other animals and in several well-publicized cases on humans – occasionally becoming domesticated. The cow and her calf will stay away a further two weeks after the birth before returning to the herd. If the herd is large, then there often is a female-led nursery. Here the young hippos receive protection and play with each other, indulging in such activities as jaw wrestling.

Lactation continues for around a year, but the calf starts feeding on grass as early as one month old, and by five months only eats grass. The first year is the most dangerous time for the young hippo, and around half do not make it to their second year.

The pygmy hippo exhibits a similar behaviour to its larger relative: the gestation period is around 25–30 weeks, with a single young hippo weighing between 4 and 7 kg (between 9 and 15 lb). The females reach sexual maturity at three to five years and the males at four to eleven years old. The timing of breeding is not seasonal, as food and water availability remain constant. Most of the breeding habitats of pygmy hippos have been gleaned from captive animals; few have been studied in the wild.[36]

The common hippo living in family pods is polygynous, and slightly more females are born than males; in contrast, the solitary pygmy hippo is promiscuous – solitary males will mate with any female that passes their territory, they are not monogamous – and shows a bias towards more males being born than females.[37] In captive pygmy hippo populations, more females are born than males, but it is not known if this occurs in the wild. Pygmy hippos are solitary animals by choice, and in captivity they tend to fight if kept in close proximity. Caring for wounds is one of the most common reasons for medical attention.[38] In captivity, skin problems associated with a colder climate are common in temperate zoos, as are diarrhoea and dental problems – for example, tusks continue to grow, and without wear and tear, they become overgrown.

Both hippo species have always been thought of as naturally 'obese', often described as 'plump, round and fatty animals'.[39] The captive population is likely to be overweight, with the average zoo pygmy hippo weighing over 200 kg (440 lb), while the few weighed in the wild have all been recorded under 200 kg, at around 150–180 kg (330–400 lb).[40] This probable obesity among captive animals is likely due to a plentiful food supply, inactivity and sometimes an inappropriate diet.[41]

Common hippos will select open stretches of water with submerged sandbanks or gently shelving banks, where they can rest all day with their heads and backs just out of the water and shallow enough so their young can suckle without swimming. They prefer to have an area nearby where they can fully submerge themselves and where the water flow is gentle.[42] During drought conditions or if disturbed by humans, hippos will move long

Mother and young hippo playing together.

distances and relocate to other water sources. When lakes were created by dams in the Hwange National Park, Zimbabwe, hippos moved in from the Zambezi River more than 100 km (60 miles) away – what is even more remarkable is that they did it without anyone noticing them en route.[43]

In 1993 the African population of hippos was estimated at about 157,000, with 7,000 in West Africa, 70,000 in East Africa and 80,000 in South Africa.[44] This is similar to a 2004 estimate of 130,000 to 155,000 and shows the population is declining or stable in the 36 African countries surveyed. Zambia, Tanzania, Mozambique and Malawi have the largest populations, while Somalia has a reported population of fewer than fifty.[45]

Fragment of Egyptian fabric with hippopotamus, from the Fatimid period (9th century).

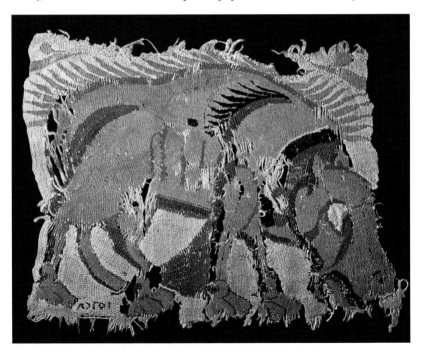

While the hippo has lived amicably alongside man throughout most of its range and history, it was particularly in northern Africa and along the Nile river that its modern history begins. The annual flooding of the Nile's banks during the early summer months allowed early man to grow crops and shift from a hunter-gatherer subsistence to agriculture, enabling the foundation of the great Egyptian dynasties spanning three to four millennia. As the ancient Egyptian dynasties waxed and waned, the hippo became more than just a wild animal; it became a religious icon and an animal of reverence.

Typical hippo habitat, Ngorongoro, Tanzania.

3 Water Horse

In Stone Age Africa, hippos thrived, and it is here where the common hippo began to make its mark on human history. The earliest archaeological evidence of humans and hippopotamuses sharing the world is dated to around 155,000 years ago. In 2001 an international team of archaeologists found butchered adult hippo bones along an old lake shore in the Bouri Formation, Middle Awash, Ethiopia.[1] These bones lay alongside human arte-facts; some bones bore cut marks and others were broken open – clear indication that the hippos were butchered and that bone marrow was being extracted. The bones of newborn hippos were also found alongside the adult bones, suggesting that it was the pregnant cows that were captured.[2]

Depictions of hippos from this era are found right across the continent as engravings etched onto the rock surface or painted on the dry interior surfaces of nooks and caves. Some of the earliest images created are found in the middle of the Sahara Desert, and date from 12,000 years ago, the early Holocene. Then the climate in North Africa, and in particular the Tassili n'Ajjer region in southeast Algeria, was moist, and rainfall was sufficient to create a network of rivers, lakes, woodland and grassy savannahs.[3] This landscape was clearly able to support a large population of hippos, although no remains have been reported. The Ajjer people left many images, which were naturalistic and without symbolism.

Around 6,000 years ago the climate had changed to one that was more arid, with no monsoon rain season. The waterways gradually disappeared, and the hippo became extinct. The local inhabitants were forced to abandon their pastoral lifestyle and adopt the nomadic lifestyle we see in the people living there today.

In Messak Settafet in southwest Libya, there are many hundreds of engraved images of animals and people, but only 3 per cent are hippos. However, in one site in the Wadi Taleschout, there is a 35-m (115-ft) section of the wadi wall covered in fifteen well-defined engravings of hippos. These engravings represent a continuum from 10,000 to 5,000 years ago.[4] During this humid period, this wadi would have been an ideal wet and verdant habitat for hippos. However, as the climate changed and the wetlands retreated higher into the mountains, the hippos also retreated, eventually surviving only in pools. The people responsible for the images were hunter-gatherers and fishermen (from 7,500 years ago), who herded domesticated cows, not the sheep and goats of later periods. The hippo engravings at these sites are more symbolic than naturalistic and show hippo cows and their young more

Hippopotamus engraved in sandstone, Bubalus period, Wadi Mathendous Area, Libya.

reminiscent of the cultural symbolism and veneration exhibited later by the Egyptians.[5]

Throughout the three millennia of the ancient Egyptian civilization, the hippopotamus was abundant and lived in the Nile river, from the great delta in the north to the great swamp in the south. To the Egyptians, the hippo possessed powerful religious significance, while also acting as a trophy and a source of meat – as well as a point of fear. As a deity it was treated with respect and honour, depicted in the hieroglyphs of tombs and obelisks, while as a hunted animal it was cruelly pursued, speared and often left to die in its own blood.

The most popular representation was the goddess Taweret (meaning 'the Great One'). She is depicted with the head of a hippopotamus, the paws of a lioness, the back and tail of a crocodile, and the breasts and stomach of a pregnant woman. Taweret was a protector of women during pregnancy and childbirth, and

Ancient Egyptian limestone relief of a hippopotamus.

of young children. This hippopotamine association derived from the well-known phenomenon of fearless female hippopotamuses protecting their young. Taweret was such a powerful deity that she was worshipped throughout ancient Egyptian history, from pre-dynastic times (3000 BC) to Ptolemaic and Roman times (AD 350). Her image adorned many temple panels as inscriptions, carvings and statues, her popularity fluctuating during different dynasties. However, throughout all the Egyptian dynasties, she was worshipped in the home, with many small statues and amulets surviving to modern times. Another Egyptian deity, Ammit, was also a composite of animals, with the head of a crocodile, a feline body and hippo hindquarters – three of the deadliest animals known to the Egyptians. Ammit was the fearsome guardian of the passage to the afterlife.

Blue glazed hippo, ancient Egypt, Middle Kingdom (2030–1640 BC).

Painted relief from the Saqqara necropolis, ancient Memphis (Old Kingdom), showing hippopotamuses being harpooned.

The differing association of the hippo with Taweret and Ammit shows that as well as representing life, the hippo was associated with death. Moreover, the hippo was a symbol of the Egyptian god of evil, known as Seth. This duality was common among Egyptian deities, and the hippo represented both a benefit and detriment to humans. For example, a hippo, once killed, could be a god-sent blessing, supplying a village with a plentiful supply of meat; at the same time, a hippo could be a god-sent punishment, as it could destroy a whole field of crops in one night. Taweret and other female hippopotamuses appeared in many Egyptian myths and stories throughout the history of ancient Egypt, acting as a god of fertility or resurrection. The association was so powerful that Taweret was adopted outside Egypt, and the Phoenicians particularly revered her.

The association with evil was represented in temple art across Egypt in the form of the hippopotamus hunt by the great god Horus. In this myth, a group of rebels have been changed into crocodiles and hippos so that they can attack Horus on the river. Horus finally defeats them, but only after they have caused much trouble.

Records from the 26th Dynasty, in Thebes, suggest that an important ritual ceremony overseen by the king and his priests was the annual Feast of the White Hippopotamus.[6] White symbolized the splendour of the sun, and represented good versus evil, and wealth. It was the colour of Upper Egypt. Countering this female white hippo was a red male hippopotamus. Red represented chaos, evil, Lower Egypt and Seth. Thus Good and Evil were represented by the hippo, though how this feast was structured is not recorded.[7]

Illustration from the Book of the Dead, Papyrus of Ani, c. 250 BC, showing in the central panel the hippopotamus god Opet, similar to Taweret. She is shown wearing a sun disc.

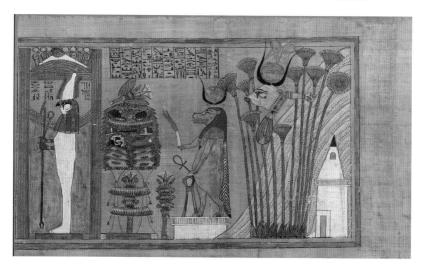

Simple clay hippo found in a grave at Hu (Upper Egypt), c. 3500 BC.

Blue majolica hippopotamus decorated with leaves, from Dra Abu el-Naga, c. Middle Kingdom 2000–1800 BC.

The hippopotamus was also an important constellation and is represented in the star charts found on the ceilings of many ancient Egyptian tombs and temples. Positioned next to a crocodile constellation, the hippo constellation is no longer recognized and may have been delineated by the stars presently forming Ophiuchus, Libra and Scorpio.[8]

Overlapping with the ancient Egyptians were the Middle Eastern cultures that eventually formed the Christian, Jewish and Muslim cultures we know today. During these times, the hippo's domain not only covered the known Nile, but was indigenous along the Mediterranean coast as far north as what is today Haifa, Israel. The hippo should therefore appear in the Old Testament, as most animals indigenous to this region are mentioned somewhere. It is therefore surprising that there are no direct references to the hippopotamus in the Bible. However, some scholars believe a beast called the Behemoth (Job 40:15–24) is the hippo. To Moses, who is believed by some to be the author of this testament, and lived alongside the Nile, this name would simply mean 'beast' in Hebrew. In the passage from Job, some of the description befits the hippo: 'the Behemoth is a strong, big-boned aquatic creature that eats grass and likes to wallow in shady brooks.' This is as far as it goes, and the rest of the description seems to describe some weird mythical beast. One commentator has suggested that the name is derived from the ancient Egyptian word for 'water ox', from B-ehe-mout,[9] while some modern interpretations say the Job description better fits a sauropod dinosaur.[10] Nowadays a behemoth denotes a variety of fictional monstrous beasts. The term 'water horse' is also used to describe a mythical, monstrous beast, particularly if associated with lakes – a famous example being the Loch Ness monster.

Across most languages, the hippopotamus is known by its ancient Greek name. When this name was first used is not known.

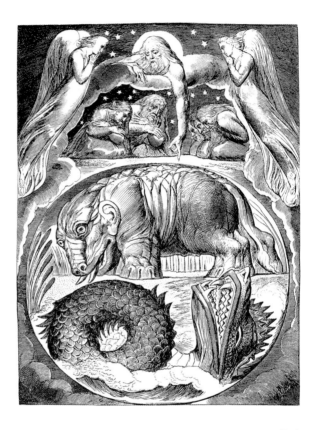

William Blake,
'Behemoth
and Leviathan',
engraving, 1825.
Book of Job, Old
Testament.

The Greek historian Herodotus (484–425 BC), who travelled to Egypt and most probably saw the hippopotamus at first hand, was the first to describe the animal. In Book Two of Herodotus' *Histories* (440 BC), it is called 'Hippopotamois', which translates as 'river horse', and is described thus:

> It is a quadruped, cloven-footed, with hoofs like an ox and a flat nose. It has a mane and tail of a horse, huge tusks

which are very conspicuous, and a voice like a horse's neigh. In size it equals the biggest oxen, and its skin so tough that when dried it is made into javelins.

It is a rather vague and somewhat bizarre description but one that reinforces the nomenclature of 'horse'. Strangely, no mention is made of the creature's aquatic habits. The Greek scholar Aristotle (384–322 BC), in his catalogue of living things, the *History of Animals*, just elaborates on the description made by Herodotus, as do the entries made by subsequent Roman scholars, such as Diodorus Siculus (90–30 BC) and Claudius Aelianus (AD 170–235). The historian Tacitus (AD 56–120) calls the hippo the 'Egyptian elephant' on account of its strength. The Roman philosopher and naturalist Pliny the Elder (AD 23–79) reiterates Herodotus' description in his *Natural History* (AD 77–9) but elaborates, commenting on the hippo's amphibious nature. The large, rotund nature of the hippo was beginning to be associated with overeating and overindulgence. Pliny describes what happens when the hippo overeats:

after over-eating it seeks out a newly broken reed with a sharp point. It then presses itself against this point to open its thigh veins. This bloodletting provides relief, after which the hippo seals the wound with mud. (Book 8, Chapter 40)

This behaviour is not seen in the wild, but the idea could have some foundation in reality – most bull hippos are covered in scars from fighting, and these scars and healing wounds attract mud as the skin is no longer smooth. Pliny's observation was revived by the French naturalist Georges-Louis Leclerc, Comte de Buffon (1707–1788), who in his *Histoire naturelle* embellishes the story by increasing the vigour with which the hippo skewers itself – using a sharp-pointed rock, rather than a reed.[11]

Pliny also includes remedies derived from the hippopotamus in Chapter 31 of his *Natural History*: he describes how the hide, once reduced to ash, can be used to cure inflamed tumours and alopecia, and act as an aphrodisiac. The fumes from burning its fat or dung will cure cold agues, and its testis, taken in water, will cure snakebites.

It is odd that the Roman naturalists and scholars chose to embellish the description of Herodotus, instead of deriving their own views, as they most likely observed the hippo in Rome, where it was imported for entertainment at the many games and festivals. Shipping them across the Mediterranean from Alexandria was not easy, but they were displayed by several emperors – for example, by Augustus (63 BC–AD 14) following his triumph over Cleopatra. Others were Antoninus Pius (AD 86–161), Commodus (AD 161–92), Heliogabalus (AD 204–22) and Gordian III (AD 225–44). These festivals could be bloodthirsty occasions: for one such festival in AD 240, 2,000 gladiators, seventy lions, forty wild horses, thirty elephants, two leopards, twenty wild asses, nineteen giraffes, ten antelope, ten hyenas, ten tigers, one hippopotamus and one rhinoceros were slaughtered. The Roman consul Cassius Dio (*c.* 165–after AD 229) tells us that Emperor Commodus, a marksman with spear and bow, personally killed five hippos, two elephants, a rhinoceros and a giraffe in one show lasting two days.[12] To commemorate these games, a hippo was often depicted on the reverse of coins. One such coin is the brass sestertius struck in AD 248, which depicts the head of the empress Otacilia Severa on one side and a hippopotamus on the reverse. These were struck to commemorate the secular games celebrating the 1,000th anniversary of Rome, for which the hippo was shown in the amphitheatre.

Della Flebotomia.

Chi fia ftato l' inuentore della Flebotomia?
Cap. III.

HIPPOPOTAMO

Dicono i naturali, che l'inuentore della Flebotomia è ftato l'Hippopotamo animale, che habita preffo il fiume Nilo, di grandezza fimile à qualfiuoglia Cauallo di Frifia, & è di terreftre, & acquatica natura, il quale, quando fi fente aggrauato dalla copia del fangue, và in vn canetto, ò cofa fimile, e per iftinto di natura fi ferifce la vena, e ne laffa vfcir tanto fangue, fin che fi fenta fgrauato : poi troua la belletta, ò fango, & iui fi imbelletta, fi ftagna, e ferra la ferita della vena.

A chi s'afpetta di fare la Flebotomia. Cap. IV.

Non è dubbio alcuno, che l'agente principale della Flebotomia è la natura, la quale opera per mezo della virtù efpulfiua. Poi fecondariamente è l'Artefice, il quale diffolue la vena con opportuno, & accommodato ftromento atto à tal'vfo; & à chi voleffe negare che la
fudet-

Bloodletting a hippopotamus, from *Chirugo* by Tarduccio Salvi (1642), a 17th-century medical text on phlebotomy.

After the fall of the Roman Empire, the hippo disappeared from mainland Europe and, indeed, the rest of the world outside Africa. The hippo is not completely confined to obscurity, however: travellers to the Middle East, as the Nile was known across the Arab world, not just in Egypt, would have heard it mentioned, as it was still common on the Nile. Carved ivory items made from hippo tusks were certainly in circulation at this time. Even the Crusaders might have encountered hippos in the waterways of the Levant. The hippo was certainly still known from the reverse of uncovered Roman coins. Today, both species of hippopotamus continue to appear on the reverse of coins, most notably in West and Central Africa, in countries such as Sierra Leone and the Republic of the Congo. Even North Korea has honoured the hippo, with an image appearing on the reverse of one of its coins.

These simple Roman numismatic hippo representations were the only visual images available to the medieval illustrators, and they influenced printed images up until the eighteenth century. Unbeknown to these early artists, much more lifelike images of hippos existed but were buried and had yet to be rediscovered – hippos appear in many Roman mosaics. Good examples were unearthed at the Casa di Paquius Proculus, Pompeii, in the nineteenth century. Another glorious mosaic depicting a Nilotic scene, originally from the Villa di Cassio, Tivoli, and now owned by the National Museum Wales, shows a ferocious hippo being fended off by the occupants of a typical Egyptian papyrus boat.[13]

In medieval Latin, 'hippopotamus' is *ypotamus*, which in old Middle English and French becomes *ypotame* and *ypotamos*. Norse

Gold coin with a bust of Empress Otacilia Severa on the obverse, and a hippo on the reverse.

words such as *sæhengest* and *ypmearh*, meaning 'sea steed' and 'wave horse', respectively, could be misinterpreted to mean 'hippopotamus', but in these cases, they were terms for their Viking ships. *Ypotamus* appears in texts from the fourteenth century – for example, in the romantic epic *Kyng Alisaunder* (1340). To complicate matters further, these names evolved to become *ypotanus* and *ipotaynes* by the sixteenth century. In Latin scripts, the hippo was given as *equus fluvialis*.[14]

While its English vulgar name was given as 'sea horse', or 'water' or 'river horse' – and sometimes 'sea cow' – the spelling of the hippo's specific name was not standardized, and we get 'Hippotamon', 'Hyppotame' and 'Hippopotame'. Gradually, by the seventeenth century, 'Hippopotamus' (sometimes ending in '–mos') became universally accepted.

By 1566 the name 'sea horse' had become associated with the fish, and given as one word: seahorse (the seahorse genus *Hippocampus* derives from the Greek *hippo* for 'horse' and *campus*, 'sea monster'). However, the confusion between 'sea' and 'water' horse continued: in the eighteenth century, it was proposed by

Roman fresco showing a hippopotamus devouring a pygmy. From the House of the Physician, Pompeii.

anatomists that a small region of the brain that is shaped like a seahorse should be called the hippocampus. This led to some confusion, as a well-known anatomist, Johann Christoph Andreas Mayer (1747–1801), the first scientist to describe the uniqueness of fingerprints, began naming regions of this organ after the hippopotamus – for example *pes hippopotami minor*, or 'small foot of hippopotamus'.[15]

Eventually, as explorers navigated the world's coastlines, the name 'sea cow' became associated with the manatee (*Trichechus*). This confusion in nomenclature with the hippo extended to Steller's sea cow (*Hydrodamalis gigas*), discovered in 1741 by the German naturalist Georg Wilhelm Steller after being shipwrecked on the Commander Islands in the Bering Sea. The large sea cows (bigger than elephant seals), not being afraid of humans, were easy to approach and provided passing sailors with a plentiful supply of meat, oil and skins. This resource was quickly exploited. The sea cow became extinct just 27 years later in 1768.[16] With the exploration of the New World and Brazil came the discovery of the tapir, which was thought to be a diminutive species of the hippopotamus and thus given the Latin name *Hippopotamus terrestris* (now changed to *Tapirus americanus*). The French naturalist the Comte de Buffon stated that it is similar to the hippo, except that it only eats plants, unlike the hippo, which eats fish.[17]

Terracotta Campana relief, depicting a Nilotic scene featuring a hippo, 1st century AD.

Roman fresco
depicting a
hippopotamus and
a crocodile, from
the House of the
Physician, Pompeii.

In 1772 a British naval officer named M. Whalfeldt reported seeing what he thought was a hippopotamus while surveying the coast of Sumatra, just south of the mouth of the Cawoor river. He made a rough sketch and an official report, stating that the local name was *kuda air*, or 'water horse'. It was not until 1821 that his mistake was discovered: he had, in fact, drawn a tapir – what we now call the Malaysian or Asian tapir (*Tapirus indicus*), which has distinctive black-and-white colouring. It is the only Old World species of tapir.[18]

The early fourteenth-century epic romantic poem *Kyng Ali-saunder* referred to the hippo in Old English: 'a wonder beest is more than an olifuant'. The description continues, stating that the hippo is rugged and coarse; resembles a horse, with a short

74

back and crooked tail; has tusks and a black head; and eats fruit (apples, nuts, raisins and wheat), fish and man's flesh and bones. The hippo dreads no one.

The first naturalistic descriptions of the hippo started to appear in Europe in the sixteenth century, when Pierre Belon (1517–1564), in his book *L'Historie naturelle des éstrange poissons marins* (1551), reported seeing live specimens in Constantinople. In the seventeenth century the hippopotamus and the crocodile were, by virtue of their amphibious nature, still classified as fish. It was only with the publication of the *De historia piscium* (1686) by Francis Willughby (1635–1672) and finished by John Ray (1627–1705) that fish received the definition we are familiar with today – the hippo being labelled as a beast, while the whale remained a fish.[19]

Early comparison between a hippopotamus ('sea horse') and a seahorse, from Sebastian Münster's *Kosmographie* (1550).

HIPPOPOTAMUS.

The Amphibious Hippopotamus.

'Hippopotamus:
A Sea Horse',
illustration from
Johannes Nieuhof,
*An Embassy from
the East-India
Company of the
United Provinces,
to the Grand Tartar
Cham Emperor of
China* (1669).

In 1754 hippos from North Africa were described in accurate detail in *The Animal World Displayed or the Nature and Qualities of Living Creatures Described*, written by Frederick Watson and dedicated to His Royal Highness Prince George. The book states that hippos are to be found in Africa, Asia and South America (the author considers the tapir a hippo). This detailed work also contains an extensive description of the methods extant at the time for hunting hippo for food and sport.

With the exploration of southern Africa – first by the Portuguese and later by Dutch settlers – knowledge of the hippopotamus grew, as did its commercial exploitation. When the first settlers arrived in the seventeenth century, hippos were abundant and found along all the major waterways of the Cape. The Portuguese, on their way to India and the Orient, would pause at the ports around the Cape of Good Hope to restock their ships' supplies; here they would sometimes purchase hippo meat. Though hippo meat was only thought suitable for the native Africans, the Portuguese would consume it on their voyages if there was no other meat available. Until the 1850s hippos were still abundant

Hippopotamus,
with an aggressive
stance, and
misplaced tusks
and teeth.
Engraving by
J. Wilkes, 1806.

77

in southern Africa, but after this the population crashed. All the hippos in the region disappeared within sixty years, mostly likely through overhunting – for example, all the hippos in Sea Cow Lake were exterminated by 1898.[20]

Some zoologists considered the southern hippo a different species, giving it the name *cheropotami*, or 'river hog', as they thought its resemblance was closer to pigs than to horses. For the local native Bechuanas tribe, *Kubu* was its Setswana name. The Dutch settlers gave it all sorts of names, such as 'sea-ox', 'river-paard', 'water elephant' and even *Umzivooboo*, a name derived from Umzimvubu, the isiXhosa name for the River Mzimvubu in the Eastern Cape Province and which means 'home of the hippopotamus'.[21] Eventually, however, *zee koe*, or 'sea cow', became the popular Afrikaans name. This is reflected in modern place

The southern African hippopotamus, with tusks reminiscent of a boar. Engraving by J. Pye, 18th century.

Hippopotamus
with a bovine face.
Wood engraving
from Ralph Beilby,
*A General History of
Quadrupeds* (1790).

names, such as Seacow, the Seekoei river – which drains the
northeastern Karoo in South Africa – and Zeekooivlei, Hippopotamus Lake, which was the part-time home of Dr Christiaan
Barnard (1922–2001), the world's first successful heart transplant
surgeon.[22] It was these first Dutch settlers who sent back hippo
bones and skins to the Netherlands, and it was thanks to them
that the first European zoologists were able to describe hippos
scientifically.

The Paris Museum of Natural History was one of the first
institutions to obtain an adult skeleton of a common hippo in
1820; it was described by the French zoologist Georges Cuvier,
who had already described the fossilized remains of a hippo in
1804.[23] At this time, the northern, or Nile, hippo was considered
a separate species from the South African and West African
hippos, which were named *Hippopotamus amphibius capensis* and
Hippopotamus Senegalensis, respectively.[24]

Before this material arrived from South Africa, the first scientific attempt to describe the hippopotamus was made by the

Illustration of a variety of animal features, including the jaws of a hippopotamus 'or Behemoth', from Nehemiah Grew's 17th-century *Musaeum regalis societatis*.

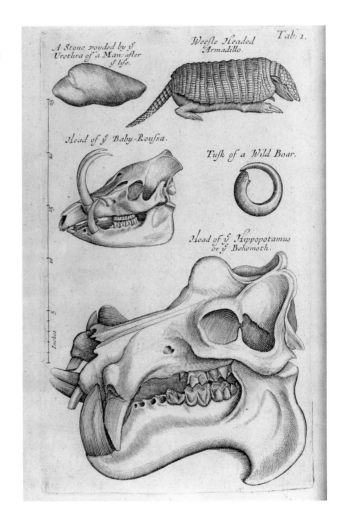

Tab: 1.

A Stone voyded by ye Urethra of a Man: after ye life.

Weesle Headed Armadillo.

Head of ye Baby-Rousa.

Tusk of a Wild Boar.

Head of ye Hippopotamus or ye Behemoth.

Inches

Comte de Buffon, the French naturalist whose life's work was to produce an illustrated and voluminous encyclopaedia of natural history (*Histoire naturelle, générale et particulière*, 1749–88). His volumes on mammals, birds, reptiles and fish mark the beginning of modern zoology. The entry for the hippopotamus is poor, as the Comte de Buffon had to rely on second-hand information. His illustration looks very pig-like, since, at this time, the hippo's closest relative was considered to be the pig. One of Buffon's aims was to classify animals into some sort of hierarchical order according to their characteristics. He believed that the Old World animals from Europe and Africa were the original forms or species and that animals in other parts of the world were the derived and diminished forms. The Comte de Buffon believed climate, food and domestication (or 'slavery', as he called it) were responsible. Using the elephant and the hippo as examples, he states that

> the earliest and greatest formation of animated beings occurred in the high, elevated regions of the north, from whence they have successfully passed into the equatorial regions under the same form, without having lost anything but their great size; our elephant and hippopotamuses, which appear large to us, had much larger ancestors during the time in which they inhabited the northern regions where they have left their remains.[25]

This notion is based on the erroneous assumption that the South American tapirs were related to the African hippopotamus (at this time, North American mastodon remains were mistaken for hippo remains), and that the mammoths of the northern hemisphere were the original larger ancestors of the smaller elephants in Europe.

In the end, the classification system proposed by the Swedish taxonomist Carl Linnaeus (1707–1778) was accepted: the hippo was given the name *Hippopotamus amphibius* in 1758 and assigned to the order Artiodactyla, the classification still in use today.

By the early nineteenth century, the natural history of the common hippo was well known. The entry for the hippo in *The British Cyclopaedia of Natural History* (1835), by Charles F. Partington, is mostly accurate and spans several pages. In it, the hippo is classified as a mammal, and a single species, albeit erroneously labelled as a pachyderm, along with the elephant and rhinoceros. In spite of this scientific accuracy the Victorian attitude towards the hippo is typical of early views: 'The whole aspect of the hippopotamus is repulsive. It has a very stupid look and yet its air is ferocious; and its mouth is about as ugly a mouth as can be imagined.'[26]

At this time, the hippo's northern range was largely restricted to both tributaries of the Upper Nile, and the last known individual in Egypt was killed around 1816. Fortunately for the hippo, East and South Africa were still little exploited by Europeans, and hippos continued to exist there in vast numbers.

The hippo was revered by the ancient Egyptians, studied by the Greek, abused and exhibited by the Romans, and observed in wonderment by the early European explorers. As colonization of Africa pushed inland from the coast to the core of the great continent, news of this large and ferocious beast created an ever-increasing interest in the public's imagination. The great European zoological institutes soon set about exhibiting live specimens in their animal collections. However, before any attempt could be made to transport such a large animal back to Europe, potential animal-hunters had to capture one alive first, and this would not be as easy as they thought.

4 The Illustrious Stranger

With the arrival of the Industrial Revolution and the Victorian age, explorers, maverick adventurers and engineers set their eyes on continental Africa, hoping to discover lands, exploit their as-yet-untouched resources and claim new territories for their mother countries. The drive to build empires by the European nations had begun. The British were at the forefront of this expansion into Africa – in North, East and South Africa, areas where the common hippo was to be found in abundance. West Africa was composed of French and Belgian territories, and it was here that the discovery of the pygmy hippo was waiting to be made. The stage was now set for the hippopotamus to return to Europe, with the first live animal about to appear in the Regent's Park Zoological Garden in London, causing a huge sensation. Its fame spread quickly around the world, ensuring that the demand for live, captive specimens created a very lucrative trade. Publicity encouraged game-hunting, a sport that has led to the decline in hippo numbers that is evident today.

Hippos had been hunted for food and for their leather for millennia, and before the invention of the modern high-velocity hunter's rifle, the most popular method was by spear or harpoon. In its simplest form, the hunt required at least a dozen men, who would usually launch their weapons at the hippo from the water's edge when it surfaced to breathe, aiming for the mouth or nose

Unknown artist, hippopotamus drinking from a stream in the jungle.

– the softest tissue, as the hide on its back was either too tough or, once pierced, allowed little success at incapacitating the animal. Each harpoon was attached to a rope so that when the animal dived underwater, the hunters could grip the ropes, and all work together to try to drag the hippo ashore so it could be lanced with spears. This was a dangerous operation which could be fatal to the hunters if not conducted carefully.

A more dangerous method was attempting to harpoon the hippo from a canoe or small boat. Often the boat would get dragged along by the submerged hippo as it tried to escape. Once harpooned, the hunters would then attempt to thrust as many spears into the animal as they could until it succumbed. If the hippo fought back, it could surface beneath the boat and over-turn it, throwing its occupants into the water; it could then attack and crush the hunters in its immense jaws. If the water was shal-low enough, the hippo could attack the boat directly and often bite it in two – again spilling the inhabitants into the water where they could be bitten and trampled. Often crocodiles were around to pick off the hunters who were unable to swim. Hippo-hunting was not something that was taken lightly, but the rewards in terms of the meat it provided were sometimes enough of an incentive, despite the clear dangers.

Many archaeological objects from Africa depict hippo-hunting scenes; one of the earliest examples is on display at the Mediter-ranean Museum, Stockholm. Dating from 4000 BC, the rhomboid schist plate is inscribed with a scene showing a hunter in a boat harpooning a hippo. This piece shows that hippo-hunting was considered the pursuit of huntsmen; by the period of the Old Kingdom (2649–2150 BC), it had become a royal pursuit with symbolic implications. Hieroglyphs depict this shift: the earliest show the pharaoh attending the hunt, with the pharaoh oversee-ing his servants, who do all the dangerous work of harpooning.[1]

It was a highly specialized procedure using a specifically adapted papyrus raft and harpoons. By the time of the New Kingdom (1550–1070 BC), depictions of hippopotamus-hunting had changed. By this time, the pharaoh was central to the scene and depicted as the sole hunter. The hunt had now gained religious significance, and the king was the god-hunter.[2] Some modern Egyptologists suggest that the pharaoh Tutankhamun may have been mauled to death while hippo-hunting, as his wounded leg would suggest.[3]

By the eighteenth century little had changed, as elucidated by Frederick Watson in his book *The Animal World Displayed*, which describes his hunting in the Nile and Niger deltas. His treatise describes the taste of hippo flesh as a mix between veal and pork. Hunting was attempted only during the dry season, when the river waters were clear and at lower levels. The main instrument used to take down the animals was a 20-cm (8-in.) iron spike connected to a thick 2-m (6.5-ft) cable, in turn connected to a long rope fastened to the boat's stern. In these bigger rivers, harpooning was not an option, as getting close enough was not easy. Instead, bait – such as a large piece of waterlily root – was added to the harpoon spike; the harpoon was then thrown into the water upstream of the hippos, and left to sink to the bottom and drift

A hippo hunt, with a man harpooning a hippo from a boat, depicted on a slate palette, pre-dynastic Egypt, c. 4000–3500 BC.

past the hippo. If the bait was swallowed, the hunters would yank the rope hard, firmly embedding the spike into the hippo's throat. At this point, the hippo – feeling the pain – would thrash around, and move away. All the hunters then needed to do was play out the rope, leaving the hippo to slowly weaken upon the bank or in the shallows. When sufficiently weak, the hunters would approach the hippo and finish it off. If they were unlucky, the hippo would approach the hunter's boat and attack it. The more sophisticated hunters would use two boats, and the bait would be attached to a harpoon with two ropes. This would allow better control of the hooked hippo, as it could then be pulled away from either boat, and safely restrained midway between them until it succumbed.

To the Europeans, it was only the ivory tusks that were of any value; the carcass would be left for the locals to butcher and render. At this time, the rifles were not powerful enough to penetrate the thick skin of hippos; instead, bullets were repeatedly fired at the hippos' heads, in the hope that a bullet would penetrate via an orifice, such as the eye or nostril, into the brain. It was still dangerous to hunt the hippo, and many Europeans and natives lost their lives doing so.

Hippo ivory was well known even to the ancient Egyptians, who made small statues and religious icons with the material and exported them to the surrounding Mediterranean, Arabian and Indian economies. Hippo teeth and ivory had been in circulation since the Bronze Age. Evidence for this comes from a fairly recent find – the 1982 discovery of a fully laden, submerged Bronze Age trading ship off a promontory called Uluburun, near Kaş in Turkey.[4] The Uluburun shipwreck dates from around 1350 BC and the vessel contained a huge treasure trove of valuable artefacts such as gold bowls and less valuable trading items such as ox hides. The ship was from the eastern Mediterranean, where the Syro-Palestinian traders exported goods to the rest of the

Hippopotamus ivory statue of a tambourine player, Syria, second intermediate period.

Mediterranean. More than a dozen hippopotamus teeth were found in the cargo, and were most likely imported from either Egypt or the Sinai and destined to be traded in the northern Mediterranean ports.[5]

Although most ivory was made into carved goods, this was not the fate of all teeth – one inadvertently became a religious relic. The Catholic monks of Vercelli in Piedmont, Italy, had, for

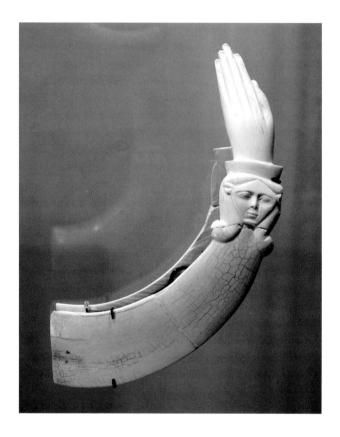

centuries, prayed to an elaborate shrine which they had created
and dedicated to St Christopher, as it contained what they
believed to be one of his molars. It was only when it was closely
inspected in the nineteenth century that it was discovered to be
hippotamine in origin.[6]

By Victorian times, hippo tusks were valued as a source of
ivory not for decoration but for making false teeth. The enamel
of hippo tusks is very resilient and keeps its colour, while elephant

ivory yellows quickly when used in false teeth. Hippo tusks are conical and hollow for about half their length; the dentine, or ivory, is of a very fine grain and is extremely strong, heavy and hard.[7] It is, in fact, the strongest ivory of any animal, and when struck by steel, it will spark. Thus, hippo ivory was sought after by dentists to make artificial teeth and dental plates – a single piece of ivory, when carved into the right shape, would make a convincing-looking denture.

In commercial circles, hippo ivory was also termed 'seahorse teeth' and 'morse' teeth. It was used in Europe to make false teeth from the mid-eighteenth century onwards, and could fetch a guinea for half a pound.[8] At this time, the practice of removing all the teeth – good and bad – was common. In polite circles, women, on reaching the age of 21, would have all their teeth removed. This was done in order to save the later agonies of tooth decay, the teeth being replaced with dentures. Slices of hippo tusk were carved into a single denture which fitted over the gums with a larger, carved front piece, giving the illusion of teeth. The whiteness was of aesthetic importance but so was their strength, which allowed them to be used for eating. False teeth made before this – from wood, for instance – were for cosmetic purposes only: the teeth needed to be removed and regularly washed; otherwise, they would rot and begin to stink.

Human teeth were also mounted in hippo-ivory bases; these teeth came from soldiers killed at the Battle of Waterloo (1815) or the American Civil War (1860s). Eventually, porcelain teeth mounted in soft, India rubber dentures became superior, as they could be moulded to the gums better, but ivory block was still on sale until 1875.[9]

Hippo ivory was also used to make vases and the handles of surgical instruments, because of its superior properties of stain-resistance. At the peak of its popularity, around 7 to 10 tonnes of hippo teeth were imported into the UK annually, accounting for the death of around 1,100 hippos per year.[10]

George Washington (1732–1799) was the first president of the USA, and one of the first Americans to wear dentures. Beginning in his twenties, he had problems with his teeth, and by his forties he was toothless and wearing dentures made of hippopotamus ivory. His two early dentures were held together with steel springs and consisted of elk teeth held in with gold and lead. His wife, Martha Washington (1731–1802), also wore dentures, and they both struggled throughout their lives with the clumsiness of them. Washington soaked his dentures in port wine to kill the horrific odour and taste of the deteriorating ivory, but this created further problems, as it stained them badly.[11] Today his dentures are on display at George Washington's Mount Vernon Museum in Virginia.

Hippopotamus ivory denture, 18th century.

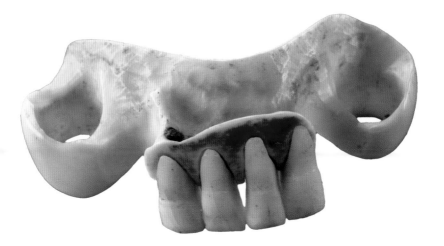

The quality of dental health in the eighteenth and nineteenth centuries can be illustrated by the following advert for ivory teeth from a French dentist, Monsieur Roquet:

Lower jaw denture with human teeth, made from hippopotamus ivory, 18th century.

He also cures effectually the most stinking Breaths, by drawing out and eradicating all decayed Teeth and Stumps, and burning the Gums to the Jaw Bone, without the least pain or confinement; and putting in their stead, an entire Set of right African Ivory teeth set in a rose-colour'd enamel so nicely fitted to the Jaws, that people of the first fashion may eat, drink, swear, talk-Scandel, quarrel and shew their Teeth without the least Indecency, Inconvenience or Hesitation whatever.[12]

Hippo skin was also a useful by-product and, when dried, was made into leather products by Africans. The Europeans eventually adapted the leather for a more sinister purpose, to make whips

– to control not only cows, but people.[13] These whips were called kurbashes in North Africa and were about 2 m (6.5 ft) long. They were made from triangular strips of hippo skin, which were coiled upon themselves. Once dried in the sun, in addition to being flexible and strong, they had a hard edge and sharp tip, which would cut skin easily.[14] The whip was used brutally, as illustrated by the following tale: one day, the Ibrahim Pasha (1789–1848), the ruler of Egypt, was passing up the Nile on his way back to Cairo and visited the town of Minya. While there, he heard how the town had become lawless and that robbery was common. The Pasha summoned a local chieftain and asked him to name all the local bandits. The chieftain refused to cooperate and was punished with 500 lashes from the kurbash.

The kurbash was especially feared when the Ottoman Empire ruled Egypt between 1867 and 1914. Winston Churchill (1874–1965) spent some of his early career in Egypt, in the Upper Nile region, and experienced Ottoman rule; he later wrote, 'Patriotism does not grow under the Kourbash.'[15] Hippo-hide whips called *chicotes* were also used for punishment by the slave traders of the Congo, as was the sjambok in South Africa during the era of apartheid.[16] Even the early European and American explorers, who relied on the local inhabitants as porters to guide them, carry their supplies and provide essential protection, used hippo-hide whips to flog anyone who disobeyed.[17]

The last regions of Africa to be exploited and colonized were beyond Khartoum, where the Nile splits into the White and Blue Nile. The hippo was still common throughout this region. The British were the first colonizers because they had easy access to the region by travelling up the Nile by rail. In the 1890s Lord Kitchener (1850–1916) was tasked with maintaining and expanding British rule over the region, winning territory from the French and ousting the Arab slave traders. Conditions were primitive, and, at times, his army struggled to survive. When their supplies dwindled, they survived for months on army biscuits, roasted hippo and aquatic vegetation. Often it was the heat and mosquitoes that proved fatal to the soldiers.[18] Kitchener succeeded and was given the title of Lord Kitchener of Khartoum in 1898.

Mr John Petherick (1813–1882) was a Welsh miner, explorer and collector – not a military man or wealthy individual, as most explorers were in those days. He explored the upper reaches of the Nile, using small boats that could be transported over land if necessary, and witnessed many dangerous encounters with hippos. When encountered in shallow water, the hippos would rush boats from the side, with their mouths wide open, closing their jaws around boats on contact and badly injuring or killing any of the occupants unlucky enough to be near them. In deeper water, hippos would dive under the boats and, upon surfacing, capsize them, killing the occupants in the same way. In most cases, however, when hippos heard the explorers coming, they would silently slink off or hide – but, of course, this did not make a good story back home in the clubs and parlours of Victorian London.[19]

As East Africa became a little more developed, travel to the region became easier. Hunting big game in Africa (which included hippos) was coming to be seen as a rite of passage for the young and wealthy across Britain and Europe and even North America, but most of the hippos were in countries under British rule at the time, so access to hunting depended on your passport. Fortunately, it still was not easy, and remained very risky. These young men were brash, confident and gung-ho, and enjoyed the thrill of the kill. The museums of Europe soon became full of specimens, including hippos, that were sent back and often mounted and put on display without any idea of how the animal looked in the wild.

The stereotype of the 'great white hunter' is typified by the self-publicist Roualeyn George Gordon-Cumming (1820–1866), the son

of a Scottish baronet and an Old Etonian, who charged around southern Africa shooting game just for sport and advertised himself as the 'the Great Lion hunter'. He describes his exploits in his book *Five Years of a Hunter's Life in the Far Interior of South Africa, with Notices of the Native Tribes, and Anecdotes of the Chase of the Lion, Elephant, Hippopotamus, Giraffe, Rhinoceros & Etc* (1850), taking the opportunity to apologize for his need to publish for the need of money, and the hope that his success with his rifle would overcome the failure of his penmanship. In the book he boasts of killing 'five first-rate hippopotami', but only at the cost of wounding three or four others.

Among the many descriptions in the books and magazine articles of this time, there seemed to be two likely scenarios when hippo-hunting. In the first, the hunter fired multiple shots at the animals, and the hippos either died later or escaped unharmed. In the second scenario, the hunter needed to make a lucky shot which would bring down the hippo, but it never died instantly, and the body was found later – usually the next day. When this happened, the hunters often left the carcass to rot. Sometimes the local tribesman were allowed to make full use of it – the skin was made into leather, the meat was cooked fresh or dried for later consumption, and the bone marrow was used for soup. The following is a typical example of this mode of hunting:

> The ball struck the hippopotamus full on the head, and he sank to the bottom, where he kicked up such a turmoil that one would have thought there was a steam-engine at the bottom of the river.[20]

Further south, with the colonization of South Africa and the Boer War of 1899–1902, the hippo suffered a great deal. The

'The Adventure with a Hippopotamus', David Livingstone and indigenous people on a boat, attacked by a hippopotamus, 1883, lithograph.

Reverend Edward P. Lowry writes in his book *With the Guards'
Brigade from Bloemfontein to Koomati Poort and Back* (1902) that
he observed an instance of some 'colonials, popping for hours at
a huge hippopotamus hiding in a deep pool'. The regular gren-
adier officers thought it was cruel and cowardly, as hippos rarely
did any harm, and they were becoming rarer year by year. The
reverend tells of how he had a word with the colonials, saying that
their sportsmanship was as bad as their marksmanship, and that
hippo-hunting was an unsoldierly pursuit, but unfortunately they
ignored his advice and continued shooting. He does not say
whether the hippo survived.

   In the seventeenth century, when Egypt was still a rural econ-
omy, the hippo was commonplace and accepted as part of the
natural environment. By the nineteenth century, Egypt had
changed: small plots of land were being bought up by wealthy

Joseph Wolf,
Hippopotamus,
1856, watercolour.

landowners from Europe and Egypt, and large, commercialized agricultural estates emerged. The hippo was then considered a hindrance, as it ate and damaged crops. The increase in the size of the irrigation networks that were needed to support monoculture also helped to destroy the hippo's natural habitat. Further pressure came from wealthy visiting European and Egyptian game-hunters, who saw the hippo as a natural target and as a resource to be exploited. As a result, hippos became so rare that when one Khedive who lived in Cairo wanted some for his zoological collection in his residence, he had to import them from elsewhere in Africa.

In 1799 *The Times* advertised the arrival of a hippopotamus in London. The advert boasted 'a live river cow of Egypt, Bos Potamus, being the only one ever taken, from the banks of the Nile and nearly the size of an elephant'. It could be viewed for a fee at a shop at the 'Top of the Haymarket, London', hardly a suitable place to keep a large semiaquatic animal. Another advert from *The Times* in 1822 stated that a

Monsieur Villette, who while resident for twenty years in the Cape of Good Hope collected the local fauna, was now exhibiting at the Natural History Museum, in the Great Room of Egyptian Hall, Piccadilly, his collection of animals which were for private sale and included fine specimens of hippopotamus.

In the USA the Ohio-based *Western Courier* in 1835 reported the imminent arrival of a stuffed hippopotamus of 'enormous dimensions' which was to be 'exhibited to gratify public curiosity' in Salem. It was 4.5 m (15 ft) in length and 2.7 m (9 ft) in circumference. While the 1799 advert was most likely a scam, the later ones refer to preserved and mounted specimens.

JUST ARRIVED,

A LIVE BOOS POTAMOUS,

OR THE

RIVER COW

Of EGYPT, *from the* BANKS *of the* NILE,

(A Species of the HIPPOPOTAMUS)

Being the only one ever brought to England, and nearly the Size of

AN ELEPHANT.

THIS moſt curious amphibious Animal, hitherto undeſcribed by the Naturaliſts of any Country, was purchaſed by Mr. Brookes, in his Travels through the Ukraine, (a Ruſſian Province) of Count RAJOTSKY, which he had procured from Egypt, by Way of Turkey and the Crimea. It is of a Species, which partakes in the firſt Degree, of the large Holderneſs Breed, in Point of Size and other Properties, ſo much praiſed, and ſtrongly recommended by the Gentlemen of that truly valuable Eſtabliſhment, the BOARD of AGRICULTURE. Several of that ſcientific Body having ſeen this Quadruped, with the higheſt Approbation, and repreſented the ſame to His Moſt Gracious MAJESTY; it was exhibited to him and His Royal Highneſs Prince EDWARD, in the Riding-ſchool, at Buckingham-houſe, who were pleaſed to expreſs their entire Satisfaction. The Breath of this moſt rare Animal is ſo perfectly ſweet, that it fills the Room with a rich Perfume; and is ſo extremely tractable and gentle, that the moſt timid Lady may approach it with perfect Safety.

To be ſeen at the Bird Shop, the Top of the Hay-market.

Admittance ONE SHILLING.—Foreign Birds Bought and Sold.

Orders taken in for all Kinds of ENGLISH and FOREIGN DEER.

In the Natural History Museum, London, a large number of the animal specimens were single-handedly supplied by the hunter, explorer and naturalist Frederick Courteney Selous (1851–1917), including the museum's hippo specimens. Courteney's bust is still on display today. In these early Darwinian times, the animals were displayed in an order that reflected Creation as told in the Old Testament, and it would be some time before

John Webber, 'An exact figure of the Rhinoceros that is now to be seen in London', 1750–93, pen and ink with graphite. Although the description given says rhinoceros, this image in fact shows a hippopotamus.

the animals would be displayed to the public according to their taxonomy.

However, in 1850 everything changed: a live young male hippo arrived in London, after successfully being transported from the upper regions of the Nile and shipped from Alexandria to Southampton, and eventually to the Regent's Park Zoological Garden. Charles Dickens called it 'An illustrious stranger'; others called it a 'fat friend', an 'aquatic pig', a 'unique monster' and an 'infant prodigy'.[21] It was the first hippo in the UK since prehistoric times and the first in Europe since Roman times. The impact this hippo had on the public was huge and easy to underestimate looking back from the twenty-first century.

The story begins with the Ottoman Viceroy of Egypt, Abbas Pasha, who wanted some English greyhounds and deerhounds. The British Consul General, Sir Charles Augustus Murray (1806–1895), later given the nickname 'Hippopotamus Murray', offered to exchange the dogs for a live hippopotamus. The Viceroy had considerable power, so any expedition given the Viceroy's authority was taken seriously. In 1849 the expedition travelled up the Nile, past Khartoum and along the White Nile; in July they found – hidden in a reed bed – a young hippo calf. The reed bed was encircling a small island or tributary called Obaysch.

Upon finding the young animal, one of the hunters grabbed him and tucked him up under his arm, but being wet and very slippery, the young hippo wriggled free and escaped into the water. To prevent the calf escaping, the hunter thrust his boat hook into the hippo's rump, leaving a scar that the hippo bore for the rest of his life. The captured hippo was named Obaysch after his birthplace and escorted by ten Nubian soldiers 2,400 km (1,500 miles) back up the Nile in a specially constructed boat; the journey took five months, arriving in Cairo on 14 November 1849.[22]

Charles Dickens's (1812–1870) version of the young hippo's capture, as told in his daily newspaper *Household Words*, is far more dramatic.[23] In his version, the young hippo's mother was killed only after being chased for a few hundred yards and being shot at several times before receiving a mortal wound. Succumbing to her wounds, she lay down to die in the reeds. It was only then that her six-month-old calf was found concealed in the reeds. The calf, surprised by the hunters, rushed off down the riverbank. Before he could get away, one of the boatmen lunged at him with a boat hook and embedded it in the youngster's back, preventing his escape. Once he was hauled on board, his fate was sealed. The hippo was still weaning, so throughout the journey to Cairo, the captors had to procure milk from the villages on the way. This proved increasingly difficult because as the hippo grew, so too did his daily milk consumption.

The news of the hippo's capture quickly reached Cairo, where Sir Charles Augustus Murray set about preparing for its reception. The hippo would need to overwinter in Egypt until the spring weather made sea transport to London possible, so an enclosure was built for him, which included a pool. When Obaysch arrived in Cairo, Murray wrote to the Zoological Society of London, saying that the calf 'is now in a yard at the back of my house . . . in perfect health', and 'It is only five or six months old and still lives entirely on milk. I think a fresh importation of cows will be necessary, as our little monster takes about 30 quarts of milk daily.'[24]

Murray enjoyed looking after the young animal, and they formed a strong bond. Murray described him as being 'as playful as a Newfoundland puppy'. Later, Obaysch recognized Murray whenever he visited him at Regent's Park Zoo, and answered his Arabic calls with loud grunts.

In May 1850 the time came to transport the young hippo to his London home. The journey from Cairo to Port Alexandria was by road in a specially constructed padded cart. The spectacle attracted huge crowds, with thousands of people lining the route, and the entourage was accompanied by a military escort. Obaysch's personal keeper Hamet Saffi Cannana accompanied him every step of the journey. In Alexandria, the specially adapted P&O steamer the *Ripon* was waiting. Constructed on its deck was a stable which was connected by steps to a 1,820-litre (400-gallon) tank of fresh water. Obaysch's keeper had to sleep in a hammock slung over the edge of the pool. The hippo and Hamet were close, and on one occasion, the hippo used his nose to tip the hammock up, turning the keeper into the water. The hippo's daily milk consumption was supplied by two cows and ten goats also taken on board. The *Ripon* arrived at Southampton on the morning of 25 May 1850, where the hippo was unloaded by crane onto a truck and then transported to the nearest railway station. Here he was placed in a specially adapted carriage and taken by train to London. After a ten-hour journey, Obyasch arrived at the Regent's Park Zoological Gardens at 10 pm. A contemporary report states: 'On arriving at the Gardens, Hamet walked first out of the transport van, with a bag of dates over his shoulder, and the beast trotted after him, now and then lifting up its huge grotesque muzzle and sniffing at its favourite dainties.'[25]

The zoo had built a special enclosure which had a large pool attached. Waiting for Obaysch was a large number of dignitaries. He quickly settled into his new enclosure and soon began to draw huge crowds. Hippo-mania swept London, and the Zoological Gardens received around 10,000 visitors per day. Visitor numbers

Obaysch and a keeper, *Illustrated Magazine of Art*, 1/2 (1853), engraving.

rose from 168,895 in 1849 to 360,402 in 1850. Even the fashionable elite of London took Obaysch to their hearts, and his popularity eclipsed that of the Duke of Buckingham, a popular socialite of the time and the main subject of gossip.[26]

The keeper Hamet left after a year, and another local keeper, Mr Hunt, who also lived and slept alongside Obaysch in his own room, was appointed. On one hot August evening, after Mr Hunt had returned from the public house, he decided to have a swim in the freshly cleaned hippo pool. He had shut the hippo in the barn before he left. Unknown to Mr Hunt, the zoo's nightwatchman had given the heat-stressed hippo access to the pool. Not seeing the submerged hippo, Mr Hunt dived into the pool and was shocked to find himself sharing the pool with an equally surprised adult hippo. This was followed by lots of splashing and confusion.[27] The keeper was unharmed.

On another occasion, when one of Obaysch's teeth was broken and causing him pain, the zoo superintendent, Abraham Dee

Bartlett (1812–1897), decided he would extract the aberrant tooth using a giant pair of self-built tongs. From behind an iron railing, when Obaysch was least expecting it, he grabbed the tooth with his tongs and yanked it hard. In pain and annoyance, Obaysch twisted himself free and charged the superintendent. This allowed Bartlett to grab the tooth again, and this time he managed to dislodge it a bit further. Obaysch, now enraged, opened his mouth wide as if to bite the superintendent in two. This finally enabled Bartlett to pull the tooth free. Obaysch then charged the railing with such force that the brickwork holding the railing protecting the superintendent nearly gave way.[28]

The popularity of Obaysch ensured that every national zoo wanted a hippo. In France, the Jardin de Paris was not to be outdone and soon procured an animal from the Pasha of Egypt which proved just as popular as Obaysch. One newspaper journalist wrote that it was his hideous nature, large mouth and propensity for remaining submerged underwater that attracted the crowds. The hippo was also accompanied by a Nubian keeper, to whom it was very attached.[29]

Eventually a mate, named Adhela, or Dil for short, was found for Obaysch and sent to the UK by John Petherick, an ex-explorer and now Egyptian consul for the British government. Dil arrived on 22 July 1854; it was around sixteen years later, in 1871, that the pair produced their first offspring. The first infant died within two days, and a second calf died the next year, but finally the third calf survived; it was born on 5 November 1872 and was named Guy Fawkes, despite being female. The three hippos all lived for a long time: Obaysch died of old age in March 1878, Adhela died on 16 December 1882, and Guy Fawkes died on 20 March 1908.[30]

The zoologist Dr E. Crisp was, in 1867, one of the first people to describe the anatomy of the hippo. His scientific study benefited from a fire on 30 December 1866 in the north end of the Crystal Palace, which housed many natural history exhibits, including a fourteen-month-old hippo. One side of the animal had been sufficiently roasted in the fire to tempt Dr Crisp and his colleagues to try consuming hippo flesh, which he pronounced to be 'excellent', with meat 'whiter than veal'.[31]

By the beginning of the twentieth century, captive hippos could be found in many of the world's zoos, but there were some people who wanted to increase hippo numbers greatly. In the USA plans were made to domesticate and farm the common hippo for its meat. At this time in America, the Wild West frontiers had been conquered and were long gone, and the population had mushroomed by millions as people had crossed the Atlantic from Europe in huge numbers. For the first time, the demand for

Unknown artist, 'The Hippopotamus And Her Young One at the Zoological Gardens', 1872, engraving.

food was outstripping its supply, and the U.S. Government was becoming concerned. Throughout the nineteenth century, the plentiful supply of cattle had been taken for granted, but now a meat shortage was on the horizon. In 1910 the U.S. Government became interested in listening to any solutions, however far-fetched. This is when the idea of farming hippos was suggested by four extraordinary people who subsequently formed the New Food Supply Society.[32] The four suggested to Congress that African game, such as antelopes, giraffes and hippopotamuses, should be imported into the U.S. and that hippo ranches could be created across Louisiana, the Mississippi and the bayous of the Gulf Coast. This did not seem that odd, since at the same time ostrich farms were springing up all over the southern USA. The eggs had been secretly imported from South Africa, but these unique birds were farmed not for their meat, but for their feathers and leather to service the fashion industry.[33]

Two members of the New Food Supply Society had encountered hippopotamuses earlier in their careers, when fighting in the Boer Wars of South Africa. While Major Frederick Russell Burnham (1861–1947) learnt his survival and scouting skills during his youth in the Wild West, it was in 1893, under the employ of the British as a scout and mercenary, and again later in the Second Boer War, that he came across hippos. He also became familiar with how the local tribes used hippos as a source of food.

The other member to have encountered hippos, Frederick L'Huguenot Joubert Duquesne (1877–1956), was born in the Cape Colony in South Africa. As a child in a Boer family, he had often seen hippo carcasses being brought back from the local rivers for food, known as *coe spek* when salted and preserved. He would sell the hippo fat to the local French soap manufacturers.

The third member of the Society was the senator for Louisiana, Robert Foligny Broussard (1864–1918). Broussard was not thinking of hippos directly – he was more concerned with an invasive plant species, the water hyacinth (*Eichornia crassipes*), a diplomatic gift from Japan but originally native to the Amazon. Once released into the wilds of the southern USA, it had grown so profusely in the rivers, including in the Mississippi, that it had formed great floating, impenetrable mats that blocked the waterways to boats and could not be cleared. He believed the introduction of the hippo would solve this problem: its voracious appetite would eventually allow it to eat the excess vegetation. This solution seemed ideal, as it would free up the waterways while at the same time providing an ample supply of fresh meat.

The Society's final member was William Newton Irwin, a scientist working for the U.S. Department of Agriculture, and also a strong advocate for using the hippo to solve the water hyacinth problem. He wrote, 'turn the plague that they now have in the South into good, wholesome flesh for our people'.[34] He died in 1911, but his ideas were published posthumously. Irwin even suggested importing the pygmy hippo instead, as it was easier to manage.

The Society estimated that annual production of a million tonnes of meat would be easily achievable. The press was on their

Henry Salt, 'Study of a Hippopotamus', 1825, pencil, pen and ink on paper.

side, the *New York Times* calling hippo meat 'lake cow bacon' in an effort to get over the public's reticence over eating anything other than the European staples of beef, pork, lamb and chicken. The magazine *Lippincott's Monthly* wrote, 'This animal is homely as a steam-roller, the embodiment of salvation' and 'a golden future when the meadows and bayous of our southern lands shall swarm with herds of hippopotami'. The *Washington Post* described the hippo as 'That plump and pulchritudinous beast which has a smile like an old-fashioned fireplace'.[35]

In 1910 a bill – known as the 'Hippo Bill' – was introduced by Broussard, to appropriate $250,000 to import useful new animals into the USA. Nothing came of the committee hearing, and the bill was never passed. If it had been, hippo meat might have become a common household food, and McDonald's might have served hippo burgers. At this time, President Theodore Roosevelt (1858–1919) had recently visited East Africa, and Duquesne was purporting to be an expert on African animals and even lectured during Roosevelt's visit. Hippos were never imported, and instead the marshes and unused ground were drained and converted into grassy pastures, leading to the beef, pork and poultry factory farms of today.

In 1909 the retired Roosevelt, a self-styled hunter and naturalist, and his son Kermit, went on a safari in East Africa.[36] The group included the hunter and tracker R. J. Cunninghame, scientists from the Smithsonian and the big-game hunter Frederick Selous. The purpose of the safari was to obtain game specimens for mounting and display in museums across the USA. They were to be mounted in realistic dioramas, many of which are still on view today. In those times, preserving by killing was not questioned. On this trip, the President and Kermit shot eight hippopotamuses, twenty rhinos, eleven elephants and hundreds of other mammals and birds – a staggering total of 512 creatures. In the account in his book *African Game Trails: An Account of the African Wanderings of an American Hunter-naturalist* (1910), Roosevelt describes his encounters with various hippopotamuses: according to him, the hunts required considerable stealth and often involved several quick shots to the head before the animal submerged. The hippo was then left to die; it would be recovered the next morning and dragged to the shore, where it would be examined. Roosevelt thought hunting hippos was not 'a very attractive sport', due to the fact that the shot and wounded hippo took hours to die, and it was difficult to tell whether a hippo was a bull or cow. He had to steel himself to shoot both male and female hippos in order to ensure that the hippo group for the diorama at the museum was complete.

By the late 1920s, at the beginning of the Great Depression, when economic stagnation began to occupy the minds of the world's politicians, the public's interest in hippos as a food source or hunting trophy – and, indeed, in general – had waned. However, in 1928, this changed due to the adventures of a single wild hippo from South Africa, who became known as Huberta, arguably the most famous hippopotamus of the twentieth century.[37]

Huberta's extraordinary adventure began in St Lucia Bay on the Maputaland coast, South Africa, when the young male hippo left his homeland by crossing the Umhlatuzana river and heading south, the start of a 1,500-km (930-mile) journey lasting three years. Today these wetlands are devoid of hippos, but back then, the area was full of them. It is not unusual for male hippos to wander from their daytime pools, but usually it is only a few kilometres when vegetation is plentiful, or as far as 10 km (6 miles) in a drought. Young males are often chased away by dominant older bulls or by cows with young male calves. At first, no one noticed the young male hippo. No one knows why the hippo headed south, but wander he did, and he left a trail of close encounters

Map showing 'the wanderings of the hippo Huberta', from Hedley A. Chilvers's *Huberta Goes South* (1931).

along the way, gaining an ever-increasing global media following. It was during the time of the Great Depression, and news of the hippo's latest sightings and escapades became popular across Europe and the USA, as he was seen as a symbol of independence and freedom.

The Zululand coast south towards Durban was largely swampland and sugar cane plantations, an ideal habitat for Huberta to hide in and from which to source food. To the migrant Indian workers employed on the plantations, the unexpected appearance of a hippo was most frightening, while to the native Zulus, the appearance of Huberta was spiritual and represented the return of the spirit Tshaka. This reverence gave Huberta protection as he travelled ever further south. Huberta gained notoriety due to his nocturnal inquisitiveness, finding horses and unusual noises especially attractive. One night, when a brass band was

Illustration of a hippo in Theodore Roosevelt's hunting book of 1910.

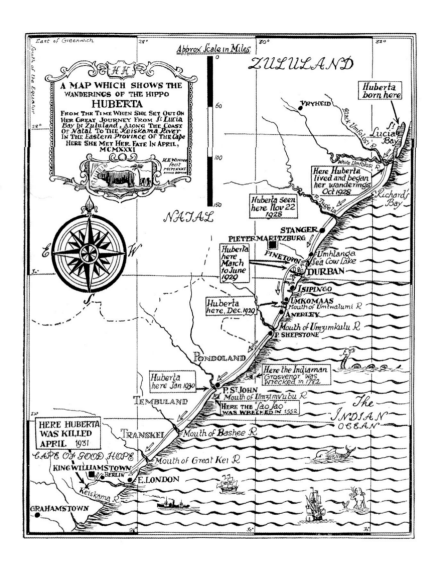

East of Greenwich

28°

30°

32°

South of the Equator

ZULULAND

Approx Scale in Miles

0

60

100

150

🎀 H H 🎀

A MAP WHICH SHOWS THE
WANDERINGS OF THE HIPPO
HUBERTA
FROM THE TIME WHEN SHE SET OUT ON
HER GREAT JOURNEY FROM St LUCIA
BAY IN ZULULAND, ALONG THE COAST
OF NATAL TO THE Keiskama RIVER
IN THE Eastern Province OF THE Cape
HERE SHE MET HER FATE IN APRIL,
MCMXXXI

H.E WINDER
fecit
MCMXXXI

VRYHEID

Huberta
born here

St
Lucia
Bay

Black Umfolosi R.

White Umfolosi R.

Here Huberta
lived and began
her wanderings
Oct 1928

Richard's
Bay

Tugela R.

NATAL

Huberta seen
here Nov 22
1928

STANGER

PIETERMARITZBURG

Huberta
here
March
to June
1929

PINETOWN

Umhlanga
Sea Cow Lake

DURBAN

ISIPINGO

Huberta
here, Dec.1929

UMKOMAAS
Mouth of Umtwalumi R.

ANERLEY

Mouth of Umzimkulu R.
P. SHEPSTONE

PONDOLAND

Huberta
here Jan 1930

Here the Indiaman
Grosvenor was
Wrecked in 1782

P. St JOHN
Mouth of Umzimvubu R.
HERE THE Sao Sao
WAS WRECKED IN 1552

The
INDIAN
OCEAN

TEMBULAND

HERE HUBERTA
WAS KILLED
APRIL 1931

TRANSKEL

Mouth of Bashee R.

CAPE OF GOOD HOPE

KINGWILLIAMSTOWN

BERLIN

Mouth of Great Kei R.

E.LONDON

Keiskama R.

GRAHAMSTOWN

rehearsing Tchaikovsky's 1812 Overture in a hut made of cane,
Huberta burst in through one of the walls, scattering the players,
who panicked on seeing his huge head and gigantic jaw appearing
out of nowhere.

By June 1929 Huberta had reached Sydenham, north of Durban,
where he destroyed a large cabbage patch. Huberta's progress

'The Locomotive Nudged her Gently with the Cow-catcher', illustration from Hedley A. Chilvers's *Huberta Goes South* (1931).

south was hindered by the city itself, and he spent a couple of months skirting Durban. Sightings were common, and his progress was reported in great detail in the local and national press; Huberta was now becoming a national celebrity. By December the hippo was many miles south of Durban, traversing a coastline that was dotted with shipwrecks dating back to the sixteenth century. On the way, Huberta was spotted by various estate owners and was even found asleep across a railway line.

By April 1931 Huberta had skirted East London on South Africa's southeast coast and had arrived in King William's Town, an area full of wetlands and a perfect habitat for hippos. Unfortunately, it was here in the Keiskamma river that Huberta met his tragic demise. Three local men ignorant of Huberta's fame had fired several shots at him while he was submerged in deep water. Each time Huberta rose, they fired, and after the fourth round, he was badly wounded. The next day, they returned and fired a further two shots which finally killed him. Soon rumours began to circulate that it was Huberta who had been shot, which triggered a public outcry that soon spread across South Africa and the rest of the world.

A few weeks later, the three responsible farmers walked into the magistrate's court in King William's Town and confessed to the killing. The case went to a higher court, and they were charged with killing royal game without a licence. The older of the accused farmers said in his defence that, being illiterate, he had not heard of Huberta and knew nothing of his fame. Each farmer was fined £25. The remains of Huberta were sent to a London taxidermist and, once mounted, returned to the local Amathole Museum in King William's Town, where he can still be found today.

After a long period of calm, the hippo re-emerged in Africa, first as a ferocious wild beast to be feared, and then as a resource providing hide, flesh and ivory. With the discovery of the pygmy hippo, public perceptions changed, and hippos were finally seen in a friendlier light, winning a positive place in people's hearts. Their gentleness became apparent when they were publicly exhibited at zoos, where most hippos spent the day content to bathe in their pools. The many factors which delayed the appearance of the common hippo in captivity – its size, retreating geographical habitat and need for a semiaquatic living space – slowed its representation in art, literature and music. Imagine how different its history would have been if it had survived the Ice Age and remained endemic throughout Europe, or what William Shakespeare would have made of its habits and appearance. Its arrival in Victorian Europe did cause a stir, and it is from this point on that the common hippo looms large in popular culture.

5 The Good, the Bad and the Ugly

The hippopotamus has been a cultural image throughout human history, beginning with the Stone Age cave art and petroglyphs found across Africa. Later, the ancient Egyptians depicted the hippo in its natural Nilotic environment and as a religious figure, in paintings, ceramics and carved ivory forms. With a brief appearance in Greek and Roman times, it then disappeared from recorded history and created little cultural impact. During the seventeenth and eighteenth centuries, an interest in the natural world and in the hippopotamus was rekindled. This was followed by the Victorians, who exemplified the pioneering spirit and chose to illustrate the hippo, red in tooth and claw, overturning boats and biting people in two. In stark contrast, in contemporary literature, it is seen as clumsy and stupid.

Even though the hippopotamus has long been known to people in Africa, there are few records of its cultural or religious significance other than in ancient Egypt. The following tale has been told and retold orally, and comes from the San people of South Africa.[1]

> When God created the animals, the hippo saw his reflection in the water and was not pleased at what he saw.
>
> 'Oh God,' said the hippo, 'may I ask you to let me live in the water so that I can hide this large, fat body away

from all the other animals who are thin and beautiful? The water can hide my shame.'

God replied, 'No, hippo, for if you live in the water with that huge mouth and so many teeth you will eat all the fish. I cannot allow this.'

'God, I promise you that if you let me stay in the water I will prove I do not eat fish. Every night when I go out to eat grass I will shake my tail on a bush or boulder and make you see I tell the truth,' said the hippo.

God was puzzled, asking the hippo for a demonstration. So the hippo backed into a bush, and as he swished his tail from side to side his dung was spread all over the bush.

God was amused, but he said, 'How does this show me you are not eating fish?'

The hippo turned to God. 'Well, do you see any fish bones in my dung?'

Of course God could not, and from that day on, the hippo was allowed to live in rivers as long as for evermore, he scattered his dung on leaving the water, to prove to God that no fish had been eaten.

In the fifteenth century, Renaissance scholars rediscovered the encyclopaedic work of the first-century philosopher Pliny the Elder, and the invention of the printing press allowed them to reprint his work in 1469, enabling his description of the hippo as the 'river horse' to be popularized. Illustrations based on ancient oral descriptions appear in many natural histories of the time. The Swiss physician and professor Conrad Gessner (1516–1565) was one of the first to provide an illustration largely based on Pliny in 1551. Gessner and his illustrators preferred to draw from life, but with the hippo, they had no choice. Fifty years later, Ulisse Aldrovandi (1522–1605), professor of physics at the

Nyau is a semi-secret masked association of the Chewa culture (from Malawi and Zambia) whose major function is to perform masquerades at funerary ceremonies.

University of Bologna, Italy, did the same, and both images bear scant resemblance to the real hippopotamus.

The prolific writer and well-travelled naturalist Johann Jonston (1603–1675) published his *Historia naturalis, de quandrupedibus*, which was illustrated with detailed copper engravings of many animals, between 1650 and 1653. Plate 49 shows three animals, one a griffin and two clearly labelled as hippopotamus. One of the hippopotamuses has tusks, a horse's mane and bovine hooves. The other without tusks looks more like a bear. Again, it is clear that neither Johann Jonston nor his illustrators had seen the animal in real life.

With the beginning of the Age of Enlightenment and the Romantic period (*c.* 1650–1800), naturalists strived to represent nature in its true form; this coincided with the exploration of the African hinterland, where many new species were being discovered. At first, the artists' images of hippos were still no more

Tab: XLIX

Gryps   Gryphus

Waſſer Ochs

Hippopotamus

Hippopotamus

Two Hippos in a copper engraving from Johann Jonston's 17th-century *Historiae naturalis de quadrupetibus.*

realistic than those in Gessner's time. Published in 1658, *The History of Four-footed Beasts, Serpents and Insects* by Edward Topsell (1572–1625), an English cleric and author, includes a small entry for the hippo, entered under the name 'sea horse', following the entry for the horse. In 1667 Athanasius Kircher (1602–1680), the German Jesuit scholar and polymath, published an equally strange hippopotamus in his book largely about China, *China illustrata*. He described the 'marine horse' as 'completely deformed and horrible to look at'. In 1682 the German orientalist Hiob Ludolf (1624–1704) published *A New History of Ethiopia*. In this tome, the rotund hippo shown has a small head and a mouth full of sharp teeth, and it takes the stance of an aggressive dog. By 1694 the French pharmacist Pierre Pomet (1658–1699) had published *Histoire générale des drogues* (A Complete History of Drugs), which contains an entry for the hippopotamus as he was listing its medical uses and properties as described by Pliny. Pomet's hippo, which he refers to as a 'sea horse', is recognizable to the modern eye but is shown next to a dead seahorse, most likely to illustrate the difference.

Amazingly there is a single report from this time, published by Étienne de Flacourt (1607–1660), in his book *Histoire de la grande isle Madagascar* (History of the Great Island of Madagascar, 1661). He worked for the French East India Company and eventually became the governor of Madagascar in 1684; his description was a second-hand account, but if the hippo was indeed still extant on the island, then it was most likely the now-extinct species *Hippopotamus madagascariensis*.

The lack of live specimens in Europe at this time may account for the rarity of hippos portrayed in art, as they are absent from the biblical scenes popular in the Renaissance and Baroque periods. Scenes prevalent at the time, such as Noah's Ark and the Garden of Eden, which normally show a wide variety of animals and birds, do not show hippos. The only notable exception is by the Baroque painter Peter Paul Rubens (1577–1640). His *Hippopotamus and Crocodile Hunt*, created in 1615–16 and commissioned by Maximilian I, the Elector of Bavaria, to decorate his Schleissheim Palace, was one of a series of paintings featuring the hunting of other animals (a bear, a wolf and a wild boar). The oil painting shows a dramatic but composed hunting scene consisting of several Arabian hunters, both on foot and mounted on horseback, attempting to spear and stab the hippo. While the hippo is only seen from the front, it is anatomically correct, albeit quite small. Rubens is known to have seen the mounted specimens of the Italian surgeon Federico Zerenghi when he visited Rome and Naples.[2]

Having access to living specimens in zoos from the nineteenth century onwards has not, it seems, inspired any of the great modern visual artists to include hippos in their works. The hippo, however, does appear more often in literature and poetry.

A hippopotamid literary revival coincided with the introduction of hippos into zoos around the world from the nineteenth century onwards. Most of the published verse or prose is either comical or satirical in nature, such as 'The Hippopotamus' by the Anglo-French writer and historian Hilaire Belloc (1870–1953). A typical example was the poem 'Habits of the Hippopotamus', which was penned by the U.S. poet and librettist Arthur Guiterman (1891–1943):

> The hippopotamus is strong
> And huge of head and broad of bustle;
> The limbs on which he rolls along
> Are big with hippopotomuscle

The association between the hippo and obesity is made by the Reverend Dodgson (1832–1898) – better known as

Lewis Carroll – when he wrote the following ditty, probably inspired by Obaysch and his kin:

> He thought he saw a Banker's Clerk
> Descending from the bus:
> He looked again, and found it was
> A Hippopotamus:
> 'If this should stay to dine,' he said,
> 'There won't be much for us.'
> 'There won't be much for us!'
> 'There won't be much for us!'

Peter Paul Rubens,
The Hippopotamus and Crocodile Hunt, 1615–16, oil painting.

This verse comes from the novel *Sylvie and Bruno* (1889), in which the gardener's song above is inspired by a rather plump dinner guest, the Baron, who likes to boast about his military prowess. His boasts inspired the lady of the house, referred to as 'My Lady', to quip, 'It often runs in families . . . just as a love for pastry does.'[3] In earlier, better-known Lewis Carroll novels such as *Alice's Adventures in Wonderland* (1865) and *Through the Looking-glass, and What Alice Found There* (1871), a hippopotamus is mentioned only briefly in the former, but in the latter, a hippo character fails to make an appearance: when the Red Queen asks the White Queen what Humpty Dumpty is looking for, she replies that 'he was looking for a hippopotamus'. The White Queen continues, 'Now, as it happened, there wasn't such a thing in the house, that morning.' An astonished Alice asks 'Is there generally?', to which the White Queen replies, 'Well, only on Thursdays.'

The rotund character of the hippo ensured that it served as a metaphor for obesity. Bertrand Russell (1872–1970), the British philosopher and mathematician, wrote:

> There is no need to worry about mere size. We do not necessarily respect a fat man more than a thin man. Sir Isaac Newton was very much smaller than a hippopotamus, but we do not on that account value him less.[4]

The English poet Lord Byron (1788–1824) on 14 November 1813, wrote in his daily journal after his visit to the Exeter Exchange, London, that he had seen tigers, a lion and panthers, but also a hippopotamus like 'Lord Liverpool in the face'. The Royal Menagerie at the Exeter Exchange was a small, private zoo on the north side of the Strand. This raises the question of whether Byron saw a live hippopotamus years before Obaysch arrived at Regent's Park Zoological Gardens.

The answer can be found in an advert placed in *Ackermann's Repository*, a popular fashion magazine of the time. In the issue from January 1814, an advert for the Exeter Exchange summarizes the creatures on display. After describing the elephant and rhinoceros, it says, 'The other apartments (there were three) contain the Tapir, or Hippopotamus of the New World.' Thus, Byron did not see a hippo but a tapir; as we have already seen, the two animals were thought to be related. Lord Byron's reference to the 2nd Earl of Liverpool (1770–1828), who had recently become the prime minister in 1812, in this journal entry from 1813 could possibly be an allusion to the latter's large, tapir-like nose, rather than to a rotund hippo-like figure.

The arrival of Obaysch at Regent's Park Zoological Gardens in 1850 generated a lot of journalistic activity. The satirical magazine *Punch* keenly followed his arrival, affectionately calling him H.R.H. (His Rolling Hulk) and declaring in 1850,

> Our fat friend at the Zoological Gardens is certainly not beautiful. He may be odd. He is grotesque. He is certainly rare. He is certainly stout. He appears good humoured. He swims with singular facility; He has an excellent appetite. But he certainly is not beautiful.[5]

This piece paints a complex picture of the hippo as ugly, exotic and beastly, appealing to the Victorian interest in the natural world and in the categorization and collecting of nature. However, a few years after Obaysch's arrival, his fame had waned, his popularity eclipsed by the arrival of a South American anteater, which inspired the following from *Punch* in 1853:

> I'm a hippish Hippopotamus and don't know what to do.
> For the public is inconstant and a fickle one too.

It smiled once upon me and now I am quite forgot;
Neglected in my bath and left to go to pot.
And its Oh! Oh! Out of joint is my nose!
It's a nasty anteater to whom everyone goes![6]

The arrival of Obaysch's mate Adhela, or Dil, from the White Nile in 1854 restored public interest for a short while. Eventually, as mentioned previously, after two unsuccessful births, Guy Fawkes was born (5 November 1872); her name was later changed to 'Miss Guy' when her true sex was discovered. This time, *Punch*'s description was more anthropomorphic and focused on Dil's African origins, giving her a derogatory and stereotypically African voice typical of that era:

Queen Lioness: And how is the darling , my dear Madame Hippo?
    Madame Hippo: Oh him berry well, tank you ma'arn. Spects all de wort' comin to see dis baby.[7]

Obaysch and Adhela lived together for 24 years. When Obaysch died on 20 March 1878, *Punch* published a long 'hippo-soliloquy', some lines of which were

URM'P! Urm'p! A feeble grunt! I fail apace.
Old Hippo's mighty yet melodious bass
Sinks to a raucous whisper, short not sweet!
Ah, well I've had my triumphs, and am yet Public Pet![8]

In 1837 the American author and poet Edgar Allan Poe (1809–1849) wrote the fable *Silence*, a short, complex story set in Zaire that focuses on the theme of opposites: heaven and earth, light and dark, noise and silence. When comparing the latter silence to the noise of a storm, the narrator descends into a morass, where the hippopotamuses dwell: 'And the hippopotami heard my call, and came, with the behemoth, unto the foot of the rock, and roared loudly and fearfully beneath the moon.' Only after the storm passes does silence remain.

One of the best-known poems referring to the hippopotamus is by T. S. Eliot (1888–1965). His poem 'The Hippopotamus' explores his faith within the Catholic Church. The whole poem is littered with religious references, symbolism and iconography. He compares what is to him a dull and boring animal with the idea of the Church – likewise dull and boring – but he notes that faith in God is paramount. The first stanza reads that the hippopotamus is 'merely flesh and blood' – that is, weak and vulnerable – 'While the True Church can never fail /For it is based upon a rock.'

One final word on poetic language, the hippopotamus has, in fact, inspired one of the longest words in the English language: hippopotomonstrosesquipedaliophobia – a word used to describe the fear of long words.

Hippos are also popular cartoon characters. Their rotund nature makes them easier to draw and animate, while their large, naturally smiling mouth makes them look benign and comical. They appear in the earliest animated cartoons, especially those by Walt Disney. In a Mickey Mouse cartoon from 1930, in which Mickey Mouse visits the Congo, hippos are among the characters. This colonial view of Africa was most likely inspired by President Theodore Roosevelt's highly publicized hunting trip to East Africa. A whole troupe of dancing hippos can be seen in Disney's *Fantasia* of 1940. The sequence 'Dance of the Hours' (using music by the Italian composer Amilcare Ponchielli, 1834–1886) is led by Hyacinth, a ballerina hippo. The film *Dumbo*, from the following year, tells the story of a travelling circus elephant,

Dumbo. The circus travels across the USA and provides a good illustration of how hippos and their young were transported in purposefully adapted railway carriages containing water tanks.

The film *Hugo the Hippo*, released first in Hungary in 1975 and then in 1976 by 20th Century Fox in the USA and directed by William Feigenbaum and József Gémes, tells the story of a young hippo who has to leave Zanzibar and travel to Dar es Salaam on the African mainland to escape being slain. Here, he is looked after by the local children and after facing more threats to his life, eventually lives happily ever after with the children. The film's soundtrack is sung by Marie and Jimmy Osmond and includes a few hippo-centric songs.

The three blockbuster *Madagascar* films by Dreamworks, released from 2005 to 2012, are headed by four main characters, one of which is Gloria the Hippo (voiced by Jada Pickett Smith). Gloria's main talents are her aquatic skills and keeping the group of friends together throughout their adventures.

Over eight years from 1978, the *Dandy* comic featured Harry and his Hippo, providing readers with 'Hippobottomless barrels of Laughs'. The nameless hippo who lives with Harry is always hungry, and his favourite food is raw cabbage. In one episode, called *Cabbage Crunch*, the hippo tracks down some cabbage thieves and is left to guard all 50,000 stolen cabbages while Harry informs the police; on Harry's return, however, he finds that all the cabbages have vanished, eaten by the hippo.[9]

Another hippo well known to young children – at least in the UK – is Henrietta the Hippo from the animated television show *64 Zoo Lane*. Henrietta is a hairy hippopotamus voiced by Anna Bentinck. British children's television in the 1980s was dominated by a large, pink, effeminate puppet hippo named George – a character from the programme *Rainbow*. This soft, anthropomorphic idea of the cuddly hippo is typical of illustrated children's

Poster for the Mickey Mouse short film *Trader Mickey* (1932).

storybooks featuring hippos, of which there are too many to mention specifically. Another example of hippopotamuses in popular culture is the Moomins, a Scandinavian family of characters who look very much like hippos. They were created in 1945 by Tove Jansson, and are the subject of nine books and numerous TV programmes, films and merchandise.

For the older reader, there are fewer stories. An early example is *Giraffe Hunters* (1866) by Captain Mayne Reid, which describes the exploits of four young men travelling around South Africa in pursuit of hippos, with the intention of shooting them for their ivory. Eventually, they succeed in killing fourteen hippopotamuses, and in obtaining 700 lb (320 kg) of the 'finest ivory'. The book contains an engraved illustration of their first dramatic encounter with a hippo, but shows a tapir rather than a hippo.

The Laughing Hippopotamus (1901) is a short fable written by the American author L. Frank Baum (1856–1919), well known for his *Wizard of Oz* stories. In this fable, set in the Congo, a young hippo named Keo (meaning 'fat and lazy' in Hippo) is trapped in a pit by Gouie, a local boy. Gouie was hoping to catch an adult animal in order to kill it for the meat and ivory. Because Keo is too young and small, Gouie offers to let him go if he swears on his grandfather's tusk that he will return a year later. Keo keeps his promise, but by then he is too big to be killed and after further adventure – as well as saving Gouie's life – he is allowed to go free.

'The Tale of Hippo, the Hippopotamus' by Ellen Velvin (1902), a writer and Fellow of the London Zoological Society, tells of how a male hippo eats and destroys a corn crop and how the farmer and his men eventually kill the hippo by plunging a harpoon into his eye and through to his brain. As one reviewer wrote, 'there is no maudlin sentimentality' about these tales.[10] They are quite accurate and full of facts about the biology and behaviour of hippos and for the young adult reader, quite educational. Ellen Velvin was keen to highlight the cruelty man dealt out to animals.

Humbo the Hippo and Little-Boy-Bumbo is told and colourfully illustrated by Erick Berry (1932). It tells the story of the friendship that develops between a baby hippo 'with loose pinky-grey, wrinkly skin' and a young native boy in Africa. It tells of their adventures as they set off to buy bananas in the local village; it is a charming tale but portrays an old-fashioned stereotypical view of native Africans.

This view is repeated in the *Adventures of Tintin in the Congo* by Hergé (1931 and revised 1946). Tintin goes big-game hunting with his rifle and dog Snowy. He encounters a range of large game mammals, such as elephants, rhinos, water buffalo and giraffes, all of which are portrayed as threats requiring shooting. However, the encounter with a hippo is more benign and begins with Tintin falling off a cliff while fighting a villain, but his fall is broken when he lands on a hippo's back. The fate of the villain is different, as he falls instead into the crocodile-infested water and is presumably eaten. Tintin, meanwhile, safely returns to the bank by bouncing off the surprised hippo's back.

The White Hippo (1980) was Alexander McCall Smith's first children's book, written while he lived in Swaziland; it is about an albino hippo and is set in the Gambia, West Africa. The first line of the book starts

> Everyone knows that hippopotamuses are grey. Or rather if you think about it, greyish brown, or brownish black. In other words, they are the colour of mud, which is what hippos are said to like most.

Of course, the hippo in this story, Seijo, is white. The story starts with the villagers' maize crop being damaged by a hippo, so they

A fierce-looking hippo, or Tapir. Illustration from *Giraffe Hunters* (1866).

meet and decide to kill the intruder. Then one night, while waiting with their spears, they see the white hippo and, perceiving it to be a special visitor, do not spear the beast, deciding instead to share their village with Seijo. Seijo later repays their kindness by killing a crocodile that preys on unwary villagers. The fame of the white hippo spreads and it gains a supernatural status. This unfortunately attracts the attention of a white hunter, who eventually succeeds in killing the hippo – a rather sad ending to a largely uplifting tale. The book ends by telling the reader that Seijo's tale is immortalized in a song sung by people across the Gambia.

Huberta Goes South (1932) by Hedley Chilvers is a non-fiction account of the escapades experienced by the hippo Huberta, as he wanders down the southeastern tip of Africa. Huberta's tale also gets a brief retelling in the novel *Ultramarine* (1933) by the English poet and novelist Malcolm Lowry. The novel is a contemporary tale, told through the colourful voice of a sailor, of a young man's induction into the merchant navy.

A novella called *Down the Rabbit Hole* (2012), by the Mexican author Juan Pablo Villalobos, is one of the few stories that involves the pygmy hippo. In this story, the main character is a young boy named Tochtli (meaning 'rabbit' in Nahuatl, Mexico's main indigenous language), who lives with his father Yolcaut (meaning 'rattlesnake'), a wealthy drug baron. The pair live in a fortified villa, where the boy views murder and violence as an everyday occurrence. When his father asks him what he wants as a present, Tochtli replies 'a Liberian Pygmy Hippopotamus'. Escaping trouble, they fly to Monrovia, the Liberian capital, and with local help capture a pair of pygmy hippos from the nearby forest. As preparations are made to ship them illegally back to Mexico, the hippos become ill, and Yolcaut has them shot in front of the boy. It is a messy event and deeply affects Tochtli. The story ends back home in Mexico with the arrival of a large parcel containing the mounted heads of the two pygmy hippos – the male, called Louis XVI, and the female, Marie Antoinette of Austria, both historical characters who were guillotined. As the book's cover blurb says, 'A pint-size novel about innocence, beastliness and a child.'

A Hippo Love Story (2014) by Karen Paolillo tells of the author's first encounters with a group of Zimbabwean hippos and how she falls in love with them and with her husband. The narrative provides lots of interesting facts about hippo biology and behaviour. Eventually, Karen builds up a rapport with the hippo groups and with certain individuals, allowing her to observe them up close. Gradually, the story descends into doom and gloom, as the hippos suffer through natural disasters such as a drought and flood. Once these have passed, the threat from humans escalates, first from the local commercial game-hunters and then as law and order disintegrates during the Zimbabwean land grabs of 2000 onwards. Thankfully, through the heroic efforts of Karen and her husband, the hippos survive. The Turgwe Trust she founded still supports the hippos to this day.

Terry Pratchett (1948–2015), in his Discworld series, created two hippos: Roderick and Keith. These elderly hippos play an important symbolic role as heraldic symbols of the city of Ankh-Morpork, where their continued presence is important to everyone's well-being, just as the continued presence of ravens at the Tower of London is thought to protect the City, or the Swans of Brayford Pool are associated with Lincoln.[11]

Fictional works use the hippo in their titles metaphorically. Recent titles include *The Blue Hippopotamus: A Semi-autobiographical Novel as Told by Earle Porlock* (2012), by the scientist Paul Ehrlich; the German novel *Selbstporträt mit Flusspferd* (Self-portrait with Hippo, 2015) by Arno Geiger concerns the difficulty of growing up in an incomprehensible world, while the fictional work *The Hippopotamus* (1994) by Stephen Fry, about a man named Ted

Wallace whose nickname is the Hippopotamus and who enjoys a life of hedonism and vice, is being made into a film.

The hippopotamus is not an animal that inspires musicians, and there are only about thirty songs featuring hippos listed on the Internet. By far the best-known song in the UK is 'The Hippopotamus Song', written by the British comedy duo Michael Flanders and Donald Swann. In the USA, there is a song associated with Christmas festivities entitled 'I want a Hippopotamus for Christmas', sung originally by Gayla Peevey in 1953, when she was ten years old. The song was adopted by Gayla's local Oklahoma City zoo for a campaign to raise money for the zoo and buy her a hippo for Christmas. On Christmas Eve, the baby hippo, Matilda, was born at the zoo and delivered to Gayla the next day. Gayla then donated the hippo to the zoo, where it lived for forty years, a story that has captured the hearts of the American public.

The symbolic hippo appears in many guises. It is used commercially as a magazine title – *The Hippo Collective*, published in San Francisco – and 'Hippopotamus' is the name of a chain of French grill restaurants with over 170 sites worldwide (why the chain is not called *hippopotame* is a mystery). In the UK, the Fat Hippo Restaurant, which serves similar food to Hippopotamus in France is unique to Newcastle-upon-Tyne. In South Africa, Hippo is a large insurance company. There are around 370 companies in the UK associated with the name hippo, such as the Pink Hippo Day Nursery and Pre-school Ltd, the Purple Hippo Consultancy Service Ltd and the Pygmy Hippo Ltd. Only three use the full name, such as the Hungry Hippopotamus Ltd of Oxford Street, London.

The hippo is used as a mascot in sport. In the UK, the mascot of Stoke City football club is a large Wedgwood-blue hippopotamus called Pottermus Hippo, and he has a companion called Mrs Pottermus. The Wedgwood pottery is based in the town, and a hippopotamus was chosen not because of the creature but because its name includes the word 'pot', matching Stoke City's nickname of the 'Potters'. In the city of Hutto, Texas, the high school and its football team have a hippopotamus mascot, inspired by a local legend of 1915 when the town was visited by a hippo that had escaped from a refuelling circus train. After much coaxing, the hippo was eventually persuaded to return to the train, restoring Hutto to its former tranquillity.

The hippopotamus, with its semiaquatic habits, has inspired a few ship names – the largest, in the Indian navy, is INS *Jalashwa*, a modern amphibious assault ship weighing around 17,000 tonnes. *Jalshaw* is Sanskrit/Hindi for 'hippopotamus'. Apart from the fact that the ship is amphibious, the name was chosen because the hippo is ferocious against an intruder, while at rest it is calm and composed. The Nigerian navy has four warships

Ugandan postage stamps showing hippopotamuses, 2013.

Coin from the Gambia, made by the Royal Mint, showing a hippopotamus on the reverse side, 1970.

named after the hippopotamus in the main local languages; they are NNS *Erinomi* (Yoruba), NNS *Dorina* (Hausa), NNS *Otobo* (Idoma, Ijaw, Igbani and Kalabari) and NNS *Enyinmiri* (Igbo). In 1816 the French navy listed a corvette of 800 tonnes named *Hippopotame*, while in the 1940s the French merchant navy named one of its tugs *Hippopotame*. This idea of the hippo as a beast of strength has been carried on by South Africa's navy, who have a tug called *Imbuvu*, meaning 'hippo'. There are no Royal Navy ships named after the hippo as such, but there have been ten ships (from 1626 to 1880) and one submarine (1932) called the *Sea Horse*, harking back to the Vikings who named their ships thus.

African countries are particularly fond of using the hippo on their banknotes and stamps. In East and South Africa, it is the common hippo, while in West and central Africa, it is the pygmy hippopotamus.

Hippos are popular subjects for sculptors and potters, and many of the world's finest gold- and silversmiths include hippos in their repertoire. The Russian company Fabergé has created many hippopotamus sculptures of jade, eight of which are in the Royal Collection of Queen Elizabeth II. The Zimbabwe-born

138

sculptor Patrick Mavros is renowned for his impressive silver sculptures of game animals, in particular, the hippopotamus. His beautiful pieces show his appreciation and love of these animals. The British artist Suzie Marsh is also well known for her life-size sculptures of hippos. A whole porcelain dinner service of 114 pieces, all with hand-painted scenes of hippos from photos taken at 101 zoos in 33 countries, has been produced in Denmark. All these items are something the members of Hippolotofus, the international hippo appreciation society, would love to own.

The return of the hippo in the fifteenth century had its immediate impact on visual art, but its presence took time to filter into the fields of poetry and literature. It is its comedic and rotund look that seemingly give the hippo its most redeeming features to the modern public. In parallel, the hippo's cultural impact changed with the various patterns of empire, patronage and finally the modern-day interest in the collecting of ornamental animal imagery. More importantly for both species – the common and pygmy hippopotamus – is their appearance in the zoos and

Hippothames, a 21-m-long wooden sculpture created by the Dutch artist Florentijn Hofman for the Totally Thames Festival, London, September 2014.

Nephrite carving, set with rubies and gold hooves, Fabergé, St Petersburg, 1907–17.

Hippo Ballerina, bronze sculpture by the Danish artist Bjørn Okholm Skaarup, New York.

animal parks around the world, for it is through captive populations that we have learnt how to care for and breed these giant herbivores. Their survival in the wild is now dependant on the commercialization of this public affinity for the hippo. As tourists visit Africa to view its wildlife, a pod of wallowing common hippos is an expected sight. The management of these expectations by the safari parks ultimately ensures the protection of the hippo – first from indiscriminate hunting and, second, by preserving its habitat, by irrigating waterways during drought and providing extra fodder when grazing is scarce. For the shy pygmy hippo, it is different, and only the creation of nature reserves will ensure its survival in the wild. The story of how the hippo became a common sight in our zoos is one of determination and exploitation by a few individuals. How hippos rely on man for protection is another and reflects our common attitudes to the value of a species that the local inhabitants see as a nuisance rather than an asset.

6 The Modern Hippo

Through the efforts of commercial animal collectors of the twentieth century, both species of hippos were captured from the wild and exported to zoos and circuses around the globe. The commercial exploitation of these large, semiaquatic and herbivorous animals, and their transport across the world, took a good deal of determination and imagination. The demand for wild-caught animals soon disappeared with the advent of the world wars, which shifted people's thoughts to other matters, and successful breeding programmes in zoos. Today hippos are protected in wildlife sanctuaries and have a positive future before them.

By the mid-nineteenth century simply shipping hippo tusks, teeth, hides and bones back to Europe and the USA was not profitable enough – the collectors, scientists and showmen wanted live specimens. It took extraordinary effort to bring Obaysch to Europe, as mentioned previously, and it was only achieved through state sponsorship by the Pasha of Egypt. At this time, a new breed of animal-hunters appeared on the horizon, hunters who were not interested in shooting and killing, but in capture and export. These self-funding entrepreneurs realized there was money to be made, not from killing but from selling animals to the world's zoos and circuses.

In colonial Africa, it was easy to gain permission to capture and export any animal one wished to, as they were considered so plentiful, and the idea of wildlife conservation – either legally or morally – was not something that was taken seriously until a century later. In just a few weeks, an animal-hunter with a team of locals could easily catch many hundreds of small animals, birds and reptiles, which could then be shipped quickly and directly to zoos anywhere in the world – quarantine was still a distant condition of import. Most of the caught animals were easy to feed and could tolerate cramped shipping conditions. However, as the zoos filled with exotic birds and small mammals from all over the globe, the public increasingly demanded bigger, rarer and more exotic flora and fauna. The common hippo was one such animal, as Obaysch at Regent's Park Zoological Gardens in London had shown.

One of the most successful animal importers was Carl Hagenbeck (1844–1913) of Hamburg, Germany. During his career, he supplied the world with a prodigious number of animals, which included 1,000 lions, 300 elephants, 150 giraffes and more than 100,000 birds. He was one of the first to bring both the common

Early 20th-century image of a hippo from the *Encyclopaedia Britannica,* 11th edition.

and pygmy hippos back alive, in each case using the skills of local tribes to obtain his specimens.

Catching live common hippos required extra care, not brute force. In Africa, for example, the Havati people (meaning 'water hunters') were different from other tribes, because they were all strong swimmers and, importantly, knew how to catch hippos. They knew that the best time to attempt capture was during the hottest part of the day, when the hippos were at their most docile. Their methods were simple: two or three members of the group would launch their harpoons at the chosen beast (usually a juvenile). To each harpoon was attached rope, which in turn was bound to the hunter. These ropes prevented the harpooned hippo escaping and allowed the rest of the hunters to swim out in the water to surround the hippo quickly and pull it ashore. Once ashore, it would be overpowered. In most cases, the harpoon wounds would heal before the hippo arrived at its destination, but sometimes this method of capture was fatal, since the wounds might fail to heal or the trauma of capture might be too much for the young animal.

Carl Hagenbeck eventually adopted a more ingenious scheme, using a concealed pit.[1] Every evening, hippos leave the water to travel inland to feed and graze. If a female hippo has a calf, she will protect it by letting it trot in front. Thus by digging and covering a pit along the route to the grazing area, any young hippo in front of its mother would fall into the trap unseen and disappear from view. The terrified and confused mother would then usually turn and run away, leaving the young hippo to be recovered later in daylight. Sometimes a lion would find the hippo before the hunters, and nothing but skin and bones would be left; sometimes the young hippo died of the shock, and the locals would be allowed to eat it. In the majority of cases, however, it was perfectly fine and unharmed.

If the hippo was unhurt, the next step was to extract it from the pit. The hippo first had to be bound – this was not simple to do, because as soon as the young hippo was stressed, it would sweat profusely, which made it slippery and slimy, causing any ropes to slip off. The captors would construct an A-frame at the front of the pit and secure a rope around the animal's neck and front legs. Then around twenty men would haul the animal up off its front feet. Next others would jump into the pit and secure the hippo's back legs and jaws. Once firmly bound, the A-frame was removed and a slope dug into the front of the trap. The hippo was then placed on a litter made of stout branches and carried up the slope. A young hippo could weigh around half a tonne and sometimes needed to be carried several miles to the nearest river, where a waiting barge would collect and transport it. In the East African Rift Valley, this was not always possible, so Herr Hagenbeck had

Hippo in the long grass, Okavango, 2011.

An early French illustration of the pygmy hippopotamus from *Recherches pour server à l'historie naturelle des mammiféres* (1868–74), vol. II, by M. H. Milne Edwards.

to haul his catches over land. This was across the Sahara Desert to Atbara, Sudan, a city on the Nile and a major railway hub.

To transport his menageries of captured animals across the desert required a camel train consisting of around 100 camels and 150 cattle. The caravan would travel at night, when the temperatures were cooler and the fierce sun was absent. The large animals such as giraffes were driven by three attendants, while an elephant would require up to four attendants. The younger and smaller lions, panthers, baboons and birds were placed in cages that were carried on the camels' backs.[2] To transport a hippo required two camels. The cage containing the hippo was hung from two stout poles suspended between each camel. Another six or eight camels carried water, which was used to fill an oxhide bath for the hippo to relax in during the daytime when at rest. The water would be refreshed every 100 km (60 miles) or so at each of the oases on the way. Another essential component of the caravan was hundreds of sheep and goats, who supplied the milk for the calf and other young animals. Other sheep provided meat for the captured carnivores.

The journey usually took around five to six weeks and on reaching Atbara, the animals were sent by train to Suez, whence they would be transferred to steamers for India or Asia. Others would travel by train to Alexandria, whence they were shipped across the Mediterranean to Trieste, Genoa or Marseilles, to be further transported by train to Hamburg, the base of Hagenbeck – a total journey of around three months. In 1908 three hippos were transported by this method to Germany. Records show that once in captivity, they each required 4.5 kg (10 lb) of crushed oats, 2–3 kg (4–6 lb) of bran, 7 kg (16 lb) of rye bread, 9 kg (20 lb) of grapes and 9 kg (20 lb) of hay on a daily basis.[3]

The pygmy hippo specimen, publicized by Dr Samuel G. Morton of the Philadelphia Academy of Sciences, in 1844, was probably not the first specimen ever found, as the French may have mistaken specimens for common hippo calves.[4] It was only the keen eye of Dr Goheen, living in Liberia, who, on obtaining two skulls, thought that they might be from a new species. He forwarded them to Dr Morton, who had casts made, which were then circulated to other scientists, such as the British zoologist Sir Richard Owen (1804–1892), who confirmed that they were indeed new to science. Despite the appearance of more bones and some pickled skin, many people were unconvinced by the declared discovery. One commentator in 1912 wrote that it was 'unknown and as mythical as the queer beasts of the visions of St John the Divine'.[5]

However, conclusive proof of the discovery of the pygmy hippo came in 1873, when a barely living specimen arrived at the Dublin Zoological Gardens, Ireland. The calf had been captured in Liberia on the Little Scarcies River, and sent to Liverpool by a Mr

Pope Hennessay.[6] On arrival in Liverpool, it was photographed, for the very first time, before being shipped to Dublin, where it soon died. After being dissected, the remains were mounted, stuffed and displayed at Trinity College Zoological Museum in Dublin, where they can be seen today. For the rest of the century, little more was learnt about the hippo. Some writers even speculated that due to it being so succulent to eat, it would go the same way as the dodo, and needed protection.[7]

On 15 June 1912, 68 years after it was first described, five living, healthy pygmy hippos arrived in Hamburg, Germany. By 10 July a male and a female had arrived in New York, the New York Zoological Society having paid a huge $12,000 for the pair (equivalent to around £2 million in 2016 prices). The procurement of these animals was the result of Herr Hagenbeck's determination to bring back living specimens before they became extinct. He also knew their considerable monetary worth.

The West African coastal region attracted the attention of explorers in pursuit of fame and money, as it was one of the least-explored areas of the continent, and there were many rumours circulating of other pygmy species to be discovered, such as a pygmy elephant or rhino. To find the elusive pygmy hippo, Carl Hagenbeck hired a fellow German, Hans Schomburgk, who was an experienced hunter, explorer and military attaché at the Liberian Legation in London.[8] It was a serious challenge: several other hunters had spent years looking for these animals without any success. On Schomburgk's first expedition in the rainy season, although he was lucky enough to see a hippo and resisted shooting it, it was too wet to track or trap any. He returned in the shorter dry season beginning in December 1911. With a group of fifty local men, he set up camp inland, as he thought all the pygmy hippos left in the coastal regions would have been eaten for food. It was a brutal trek, and he resorted to using physical punishment to keep his team together. Eventually, after many weeks travelling up and down the tributaries of the Lofa River, he found his quarry, known to the locals as *Mwe*. Inexplicably, he shot the first specimen he saw, but then set his men to dig pits. In all, they dug around one hundred pits, each around 2 m (6.5 ft) deep and covered to be invisible. Eventually, the plan worked, and he caught his first hippo – a bull – without a shot being fired. A fence was then built around the hole, and the hippo was let out. Six days later, a cow was trapped, and two days after this, a young bull. This is where the hard work started: giant wicker baskets had to be built to transport the animals. It took a team of forty men twelve days to carry the animals to the nearest navigable river.

Hans Schomburgk managed to get the three animals delivered safely downriver to one of Mr Hagenbeck's keepers, who was waiting for them. Before the rains started, and accompanied by his wife, Schomburgk returned to his base camp and found that a further two had been captured. This time, with supervision from his wife, the two animals were transported back to civilization. All five were fed and transferred into proper cages and shipped on the steamer *Alexandra Woermann* back to Germany. Being June, the journey went smoothly, except for a storm in the Bay of Biscay. It was a momentous achievement, and the animals were visited by Kaiser Wilhelm II at Hagenbeck's animal park in Stellingen, Hamburg. These were the first of many pygmy hippos which were to be captured from the wild; it was a trade which continued until fairly recently, the last wild-caught animals having been imported to Kuala Lumpar, Malaysia, in September 1982.[9] In all, 162 hippos have been, by 2016, exported from Liberia and around 300–350 captive hippos are present in the world's zoos, with only a few of these wild-caught hippos left. Most zoo hippos are born in captivity. Basel Zoo, in Switzerland, keeps a studbook of every pygmy hippo born in the world's zoos today.[10]

Pygmy hippo, with the first pygmy hippo calf born in the USA, New York Zoological Park, 1919.

One of the early hippo arrivals to the USA in 1861 was not destined for a zoo but for the Barnum Museum of Curiosities, New York City, an establishment akin to the Exeter Exchange in London, owned by the world-famous showman P. T. Barnum (1810–1891). In advertising his new arrival, Barnum ruthlessly exploited its publicity value and gave scant regard to its cramped living conditions. He was hoping to emulate the crowd appeal of Obaysch. In typical showman style, he advertised it as the 'Great behemoth of the Scriptures'. His advertising was a great success and attracted many thousands of visitors. The *New York Times* stated: 'Mr Barnum has the greatest novelty, and most valuable curiosity in the country. No one should miss the opportunity of seeing the hippopotamus.' Like the French and British hippos, the American one – named Ondina – came with her keeper, who was employed more for theatre than as a keeper. He was not from

East Africa, as it was said he had an Oriental accent. Although the hippo was a youngster, she was still quite large. The *New York Times* was undecided whether she looked like a cow or a 'mammoth hog'.[11] It further reported that the hippo was bashful but would respond to her keeper and happily open her mouth wide for a cob of corn, obviously something the visitors found very entertaining.

A year earlier, in 1860, the showman Frank Howes had imported the first hippo seen in the USA, having obtained her from Joseph Cushing's circus in England. Originally the hippo, named Bucheet (which in Arabic means 'fortunate'), had been imported from the White Nile region and was the first captive hippo outside London. After being exhibited in several provincial zoos, the last being Hull Zoological Gardens, she was exported via Liverpool docks, on 3 October aboard the steamer *City of Manchester*, accompanied by Ali, her Arabian attendant. She arrived in New York on 19 October, where she was loaded onto the *DeSoto* and shipped to New Orleans. Here she was exhibited at the Spalding and Rogers Museum from 1 November. Her exploits were reported in the *New York Times* on 16 November 1860, which described how her owners announced that she would be led through the streets on her way to the railway station. As a result, vast crowds lined the street, making the animal nervous. In fright, she reared up on her hind legs and let out a loud roar, described as 'Ooachunckon'. Initially, the crowd was amused and laughed, but their mood changed suddenly; fear took hold, and as they surged forward, the crush threatened to harm the hippo. Luckily, the keeper calmed the crowd, and the hippo survived. Later, she was shipped to Havana, Cuba, and exhibited there.[12] Bucheet ended her days in Canada in G. C. Quick's circus. A statue commemorating this hippo has recently been erected in the centre of Hull.

As more hippos arrived in the USA and were bred successfully, every travelling circus acquired one or two to exhibit. To the general public, they were advertised differently: some circuses used the term 'White Nile Hippopotamus', as this reflected the much-publicized exploits of the European colonists in Africa, and later President Theodore Roosevelt's hunting expedition. Often the hippo was lauded for its great size and, in even more sensational terms, advertised as 'blood-sweating'.

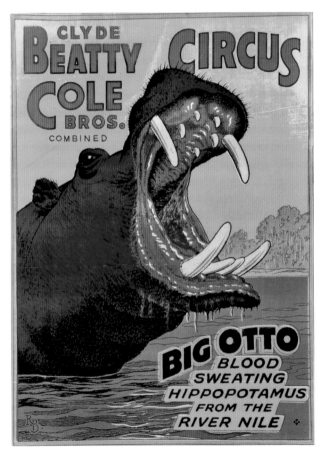

Big Otto the blood-sweating hippopotamus, Clyde Beatty Cole Bros Circus, Poster, 1963.

The travelling circus and menageries moved around the United States by train. Before the establishment of city zoos, common today, this was the only opportunity for the public to view these animals. In the early twentieth century few Americans, particularly the early settlers and pioneers, had seen any exotic foreign animals like elephants or hippopotamuses. It was not until the completion of the Transcontinental Railroad that the animals could be exhibited west of the Mississippi and Rockies. Pasadena in California welcomed the arrival of the first travelling menagerie in 1887, bringing a hippo and five elephants. On this occasion, the hippo was for display purposes only and not expected to perform like the elephants. These visits were reminiscent of the triumphal parades of ancient Rome. While it was fairly easy to feed hippos, with lots of apples and bran, they needed special railway carriages for transport that contained pools, as depicted in the Disney film *Dumbo*.

The Ringling Bros and Barnum & Bailey Circus exhibited six hippos in the twentieth century (until 1965), and one pygmy hippo. The two common hippo males were called August and Chester, and the two common females were named Lilly and Eva.

Three Victorian *Happy Families* hippopotamus playing cards.

Lotus was the pygmy hippo. Lotus was used in the show and pulled a cart around the circus ring while being led. She lived for 42 years, which is the longest recorded lifespan of a circus hippopotamus.[13] The pygmy hippo, called Betty Lou, was imported directly from Liberia in 1938 (she died in 1970) and donated by Harvey Firestone, who had rubber plantations in the country. During the show, she was paraded around the ring in her cage, which was drawn by a four-horse team.

When a circus arrived in town, good ticket sales were always guaranteed. Little was known about the hippopotamus, as illustrated in a newspaper article about a Ringling Bros Circus visit to the town of Hennessey, Oklahoma, in 1899. A local schoolteacher, taking advantage of the visitors, invited the hippopotamus-keeper to the school to talk to her zoology class. After some questions, the teacher asked the keeper how he had captured the hippo. His answer: 'Hippos cannot see by moonlight, and are absolutely helpless, so you can chain and rope the river horse at this time and if you place a bandage over his eyes he thinks the moon is still shining which will allow him to be placed in a wooden box.'[14]

Once Obaysch arrived in London in 1850, and the pygmy hippos came to Germany and New York, in 1912, vets and zookeepers quickly had to learn how to nurture and breed both species. On paper, their diet was similar to other ruminants, and they could eat vegetables, grain and fruit. Catering for their semi-aquatic lifestyle was essential; once provided with a pool, they were quiet, placid and happy. These early pools were more like large baths, given their size relative to the hippos. Captive hippos did not seem to miss their night-time foraging expeditions and were quite happy to feed in their barns. Thus, a few adult hippos made an impressive addition to any zoo, without the zoo having to spend a great deal on upkeep. If a zoo had access to fresh, running water, then flushing out the hippo pool was easy. The pygmy hippo

INFORMATION

BROOKFIELD ZOO

FEDERAL ART PROJECT·WPA·ILL.

Brookfield Zoo
poster, 1936–8.

was even easier to keep – although it does require a tropical hot-house environment, its small size makes it even more of an attractive zoo animal.

Young hippos are docile – for example, for the first two years, Obaysch would let the zookeepers ride on his back.[15] They are not so docile upon reaching adulthood, when they often become aggressive towards their keepers and will charge anyone who enters their enclosures. Being crushed by a charging hippo or bitten by one can be lethal.

In the early history of captivity, newborn hippos did not survive long. Hippo enclosure pools were designed for adult or juvenile hippos and had steep sides and deep water, which led to the younger animals drowning as they could not stay afloat or climb out of the pool in time. At first, it was thought that separating the calf for hand-rearing was the best solution. This is illustrated by the early efforts to separate Adhela from her second calf in 1871. To do this, the keepers tried to distract her by spraying water in her face; they then seized the opportunity to remove the calf quickly when Adhela dived underwater. Removing the calf was not easy, as it weighed around 45 kg (100 lb), was covered in slippery slime, and struggled and wriggled considerably.[16] They did finally remove the calf and once it had settled down, they tried to bottle-feed it with goat's milk. Unfortunately, this tactic was unsuccessful, and the animal died.

In August 1925 the Auckland Zoo in New Zealand received a young male hippo named Chaka, who had been shipped in from the Calcutta Zoological Gardens in India, via London. Chaka was imported to be a companion for Bella, their female hippo. The following year, the pair produced a healthy calf, born 28 September 1926. The birth was widely publicized by the *Auckland Star*. However, the next day, the calf was found dead, crushed underneath Chaka, and a later examination of the corpse showed that he had been fatally bitten by his father.[17] Perhaps as a result of this kind of incident, nowadays all hippo enclosures give the males a separate area and pool.

In the twentieth century hippos of both species became widespread and popular as zoo exhibits. Most enclosures today consist of large pools for the animals to bathe in; for pygmy hippos, this is contrary to their natural habitat of thick vegetation, where they can conceal themselves, but having thick vegetation in an exhibit would hide the animals from the visitors.

Many European zoos were bombed during the Second World War. While some hippos survived, others met their inevitable deaths. In Prague, four of the zoo's common hippos survived the war by being taken by their keeper to the local spas to avoid the bombing. Berlin Zoological Garden, founded in 1844, was completely destroyed by Allied bombing, and several pygmy hippos were lost.[18] Towards the end of the war, Japanese zoos faced a similar prospect, with American bombing raids of ever-increasing ferocity. In 1945 Japan's oldest and most important zoo, Ueno Zoological Gardens in Tokyo, had two common hippos: Kyōko, originating from Seoul Zoo, Korea, and her offspring Maru.[19] In 1943 the zoo's three Indian elephants, along with several other animals, had already been deliberately starved to death. The acting director Saburō Fukuda had purposely starved them as propaganda, and for him, it had provided a subtle way of preparing the public for the possible destruction of the zoo without seeming overtly defeatist. In 1945, after a huge U.S. Air Force firebombing raid on 10 March, which had killed over 80,000 inhabitants, Saburō Fukuda decided it was the turn of the two remaining hippos. On 19 March he withheld their food – Maru lasted thirteen days, and Kyoko 37. After the war, the fate of the elephants and two hippos was quietly forgotten until the 1980s, when the inhumane treatment given to the elephants was

The male pygmy hippo Thug, London Zoo, 2014.

written about, and they were portrayed as 'victims of war' in several children's books and films. The hippos' fates have been overlooked, as their deaths were seen as a direct result of the air raid bombings, rather than starvation, but this is clearly not the case. It may just be that elephants are more noteworthy than hippos to the Japanese.

Today, building a modern enclosure for the common hippo is very expensive, especially if a plentiful freshwater supply is not easily accessible. In 2015 Cincinnati Zoo began construction on a new $7.3 million enclosure for its three adult hippos. The centre-piece of the exhibit is a 250,000-litre (70,000-gallon) pool. It is lined with a glass viewing wall so the animals can be viewed by the public underwater. During the day, the hippos spend virtually all their time submerged, so an underwater viewing platform is essential if the public are to enjoy them fully. What adds to the expense is the water-filtration equipment that accompanies the exhibit. Each hippo can produce around 180 kg (400 lb) of waste per day. So without multistage filtration and aeration, the water would soon become opaque and quite smelly. Another expense is the thick glass that lines the viewing gallery. Glass has to be used instead of acrylic, which is the normal material used in sea aquaria, because acrylic soon becomes gouged and scratched by the hippos' tusks. The glass has to be extra strong and 9 cm (3.5 in.) thick to withstand a water pressure of 31 MPa (megapascals) (4,500 psi), plus the impact of a hippo travelling at 16 kph (10 mph).

Wild hippos are not only found in Africa. A population of around sixty are now living in the lakes and jungle of the Antioquia region of Colombia in South America. How they got there is a bizarre tale. Pablo Escobar, the famous drug baron and mastermind behind the Medellín Cartel in the 1970s and '80s, made vast

Hippopotamus in San Diego Zoo, 2002.

sums of money shipping cocaine to the USA. He was so successful that at the peak of his reign, he was thought to be the seventh-richest man in the world, earning billions of dollars a year. At his ranch Hacienda Nápoles, in Colombia, he created his own private zoo, and with many government officials on his payroll he was able to smuggle in animals from abroad, including elephants and giraffes. His ranch included a lake, so he imported three hippos – two females and a male. The tropical rainforest environment was so favourable that they quickly increased in number to more than thirty. While thousands of people met their deaths thanks to Escobar, it was only when he ordered the assassination of Justice Minister Rodrigo Lara Bonilla in 1984 that his rule was challenged and his downfall began. Eight years later, in 1992, he was killed during a gun battle with the Colombian police. Following his death, his estate was abandoned and left unclaimed, and the larger zoo animals were distributed by the Colombian government to Colombian zoos. The hippos, being difficult to transport, were left alone. It was not until fourteen years later, when the Ministry of the Environment began to receive phone calls about strange sightings 'of river creatures with small ears and really big mouths' that officials became aware that not only had the hippos survived, but they had bred and migrated away from the ranch. Since then, the hippos have become an accepted part of the local scenery and a lucrative tourist attraction. The Colombian government does not know what to do to control numbers: no zoos want them and controlling their fertility is too expensive. So for the time being, Pablo Escobar's hippos will continue to extend their range across Colombia, and no doubt eventually the common hippo will become endemic to Central and South America.

Throughout Africa, the survival of all large herbivores, such as the hippo, is under increasing threat from exploitation by humans, poaching, replacement by livestock, land-use change and conflict.[20] The exploitation of hippos has not changed, and both species are killed for their meat and ivory. With the common hippo, the exploitation levels seem sustainable – it occurs on an ad hoc basis, rather than being orchestrated by organized crime gangs, as in the case of the rhino and elephant. But the number of livestock in Africa is ever increasing, along with the subsequent demand for pasture. For the hippo, this has decreased its domain, as swampy areas have been drained and reclaimed. For hippos to live and breed successfully, they need grazing areas close (no further than 3 km, or 2 miles, away) to their basking pools, so if either are removed, the hippos have no choice but to move elsewhere. Agriculture and human settlements both require a plentiful supply of water, and as rivers are dammed to meet these demands, the resident hippos have to move on. This is sometimes a blessing in disguise, since the new lakes provide a better and safer habitat. The common hippo is classified as vulnerable in Africa, but it is distributed abundantly in isolated pockets in West and East Africa. Recent conflicts have had dramatic effects on some larger African herbivores like the elephant, but not the hippo – hippos spend their days in the water largely out of harm's way, so killing them for food and ivory is not easy, whereas elephants are land-based mammals and therefore easy targets.

People often mistake, at their peril, the docility of a basking hippopotamus. While many people get killed or badly injured by hippos, it is rarely the hippos' fault. The hippo is among the most dangerous animals in the world, ironically with more people being killed by hippos than by the crocodiles they often share the water with. One of the most common incidents involves upturned fishing boats. The annoyed hippo will often crunch the capsized boat – or worse, its occupants – between its mighty jaws. Apart from death, the injuries gained by such an encounter can be dangerous, as shown in a case study from Naivasha Hospital in Kenya, which describes how a fisherman was saved from bleeding to death after his lower leg had been nearly completely severed following an attack by a hippopotamus.[21] On the riverbank, people get killed or injured when they are caught between the hippo and water, or if they approach a cow with a calf too closely; often this happens to tourists or even people walking their dogs.[22]

People and hippos also have fatal nocturnal encounters. On their way to their feeding grounds, hippos often cross roads, and if there is a collision, the hippo and the car occupants might be injured or killed. A news report from 2014 told how a hippo was struck by a juggernaut lorry as it crossed the road in the dark. The body was left on the roadside, and the next day, the inhabitants of a nearby village appeared to butcher the animal and make full use of its carcass. Unfortunately, ten of the villagers were killed, as they themselves got hit by another juggernaut. Three migrants

Warning sign, 'hippos crossing', South Africa.

crossing the border at night from Zimbabwe to South Africa via the Limpopo river were killed by hippos in 2015.

The common hippo is still found in many parts of Africa, and these populations seem robust for the time being. Hippos and humans can live side by side in relative harmony, and swampy aquatic environments seem to be the last places to attract city developers. Hippos are of no threat to fisheries directly, as they do not eat valuable fish; in fact, they fertilize the waters with their dung. They are a nuisance when it comes to crops, however, which they seem to be good at destroying, but when it is a golf course or a park, toleration is still shown.

The financial value of a hippo in 2005 was around $1,500, with $100 per kg for the canine teeth, around $1 per kilogram for its flesh and $15 per kilogram for the skin.[23] The skin is valuable, as it makes strong leather, with a fine pattern, and the hide can be split into several sheets. A trophy-hunted hippo is worth more, as the hunter pays for the privilege of shooting the animal, typically

A pod of hippos basking in a water hollow, Serengeti, 2013.

a male over twenty years old. Such a hippo can make from $4,000 to $10,000, depending on size and country of origin. These figures make hippos more profitable per hectare than cattle, and in some regions, hippo populations are being managed to maximize their numbers. This, coupled with the increase in tourism to these areas, further enhances the value of hippos per hectare.[24]

While the number of pygmy hippos has never been accurately estimated, there are thought to be between 2,000 and 3,000 in Liberia, Sierra Leone, Guinea and the Ivory Coast.[25] Field surveys are improving with better technology, but even these are slow. In a recent study in Sapo National Park in Liberia involving several motion- and heat-sensitive cameras, over one month only seven images of the pygmy hippo were taken.[26] The survival of the pygmy hippo also depends on the attitudes of the local

population, as poaching and habitat loss are likely to reduce the population. A survey of the attitudes of the local people living around the Tiwai Island sanctuary in Sierra Leone found that although pygmy hippos were rarely seen, local farmers attributed some of their crop damage to them.[27] These studies show that local education programmes and monitoring of poaching are needed if we are to ensure that the pygmy hippo survives in the rainforests of West Africa. At the moment, its isolation and preference for a nocturnal lifestyle provide some protection against human exploitation, but unfortunately such small populations are sensitive to sudden catastrophic declines in number and even extinction.

Humans and hippos are set to share their futures together, as hippo numbers across South and East Africa are increasing, or at

Hippos in the Serengeti, 2013.

Sunset at
Amboseli National
Park, Kenya.

the very least remaining stable. We have learnt how to care for the hippopotamus, meeting its needs for good nutrition and an environment for it to breed in successfully. The future is bright, and as more people travel to Africa and zoos worldwide and experience the animal close up, they will learn to appreciate this unique mammal, with its split lifestyle – half aquatic and half terrestrial. This duality characterizes the hippo's history, as it evolved in Asia yet survives only in Africa, reflected in the survival of two species – one large and one pygmy. To the ancient Egyptians, it was seen as both a deity to worship and an animal to hunt in cold blood. Similarly, among the Victorians, the first modern people to view the hippo in captivity, it was at first touted as a ferocious beast to be feared and respected, but then quickly became a creature with a sentimental aura. This duality continues today as the trophy-hunter shoots to kill, while the tourist shoots their camera. It is the latter that we hope will ultimately save these unique animals, animals that – like their cousins, the whales – need humans to protect and value them.

Timeline of the Hippopotamus

20–16 MYA	8–7 MYA	155,000 YEARS AGO
Earliest fossils of Hippopotamidae appear	Hippopotamine event – modern hippos appear in the fossil record across Asia, Europe and Africa	Evidence of hippos hunted by Stone Age humans, Ethiopia

440 BC	248 BC	AD 1340	1804
Herodotus provides the earliest description of the common hippo	Hippo depicted on roman coins	First literary mention of hippo in epic poem *Kyng Alisaunder*	Common hippo reported in South Africa

1860	1910	1912
Bucheet, first hippo in the USA	Congressman Broussard introduces the Hippo Act to U.S. Congress	First living specimens of pygmy hippos arrive in Hamburg, Germany

130,000–115,000 YEARS AGO	100,000 YEARS AGO	5500 BC	3000 BC

During the Eemian Interglacial, the common hippopotamus is widespread in southern Britain

Hippo species become extinct throughout Europe

Rock painting of common hippo created, Tassili n'Ajjer, Algeria

Hippo-hunting depicted on early Egyptian artefact

1844	1850	1850

Bones from the pygmy hippo discovered in West Africa

Obaysch arrives in Regent's Park Zoological Gardens, London; he is the first living hippo in Europe since Roman times

Fossilized remains of three dwarf hippo species discovered in Madagascar

1928	1991	2015

Huberta starts trek from Zululand, South Africa

Turgwe Hippo Trust founded, Zimbabwe, Africa

Cincinnati Zoo begins construction on its new hippo exhibit

References

1 A TALE OF TWO HIPPOS

1 Claudine Montgelard, François M Catzeflis and Emmanuel
   Douzery, 'Phylogenetic Relationships of Artiodactyls and
   Cetaceans as Deduced from the Comparison of Cytochrome
   b and 12S rRNA mitochondrial sequences', *Molecular Biology
   and Evolution*, XIV/5 (1997), pp. 550–59; Jean-Renaud Boisserie,
   Fabrice Lihoreau and Michel Brunet, 'The Position of
   Hippopotamidae within Cetartiodactyla', *Proceedings of the
   National Academy of Sciences*, CII/5 (2005), pp. 1537–41;
   Jean-Renaud Boisserie et al., 'Evolving Between Land and
   Water: Key Questions on the Emergence and History of the
   Hippopotamidae (Hippopotamoidea, Cetancodonta,
   Cetariodactyla)', *Biological Reviews, Cambridge Philosophical
   Society*, LXXXVI/3 (2011), pp. 601–25.
2 Fabrice Lihoreau et al., 'Hippos Stem from the Longest Sequence
   of Terrestrial Cetartiodactyl Evolution in Africa', *Nature
   Communications*, VI (2015), pp. 62–4.
3 Boisserie et al., 'Evolving Between Land and Water'.
4 Dirk Albert Hooijer, 'Fact and Fiction in Hippopotamology
   (Sampling the History of Scientific Error)', *Osiris*, X (1952),
   pp. 109–16.
5 Nina G. Jablonski, 'The Hippo's Tale: How the Anatomy and
   Physiology of Late Neogene *Hexaprotodon* Shed Light on Late
   Neogene Environmental Change', *Quaternary International*, CXVII/1
   (2004), pp. 119–23.

6 E. M. Weston, 'A New Species of Hippopotamus *Hexaprotodon lothagamensis* (Mammalia: Hippopotamidae) from the Late Miocene, Kenya', *Journal of Vertebrate Palaeontology*, xx (2000), pp. 177–85.

7 Boisserie et al., 'Evolving Between Land and Water'; Jean-Renaud Boisserie, 'The Phylogeny and Taxonomy of Hippopotamidae (Mammalia: Artiodactyla): A Review Based on Morphology and Cladistic Analysis', *Zoological Journal of the Linnean Society*, cxliii/1 (2005), pp. 1–26.

8 R. W. Dennell, 'Early Pleistocene Hippopotamid Extinctions, Monsoonal Climates, and River System Histories in South and South West Asia: Comment on Jablonski (2004), "The Hippo's Tale: How the Anatomy and Physiology of Late Neogene *Hexaprotodon* Shed Light on Late Neogene Environmental Change"', *Quaternary International*, cxxvi/1 (2005), pp. 283–7.

9 Hoojer, 'Fact and Fiction in Hippopotamology'.

10 Ibid.

11 Ibid.

12 Dr A. J. Sutcliffe, 'The Hippopotamus in Britain', *Bulletin of the Mammal Society of the British Isles*, xi (1959), pp. 36–40.

13 J. W. Franks, 'Interglacial Deposits at Trafalgar Square London', *New Phytologist*, lix/2 (1960), pp. 145–53.

14 Th. van Kolfschoten, 'The Eemian Mammal Fauna of Central Europe', *Netherlands Journal of Geosciences*, lxxix/2–3 (2000), pp. 269–81.

15 Luca Pandolfi and Carmelo Petronio, 'A Brief Review of the Occurrences of Pleistocene Hippopotamus (Mammalia: Hippopotamidae) in Italy', *Geologica Croatica*, lxviii/3 (2015), pp. 313–19.

16 Céline Stoffel et al., 'Genetic Consequences of Population Expansions and Contractions in the Common Hippopotamus (*Hippopotamus amphibius*) Since the Late Pleistocene', *Molecular Ecology*, xxiv/10 (2015), pp. 2507–20.

17 Sutcliffe, 'The Hippopotamus in Britain'.

18 Antoine Zazzo et al., 'Direct Dating and Physic-chemical Analyses

Cast Doubts on the Coexistence of Humans and Dwarf Hippos in Cyprus', *plosone*, x/8 (2015), e0134429.

19 Alexandra van der Geer et al., *Evolution of Island Mammals: Adaption and Extinction of Placental Mammals on Islands* (London, 2010), p. 496.

20 D. A. Burney et al., 'A Chronology for Late Prehistoric Madagascar', *Journal of Human Evolution*, xlvii/1 (2004), pp. 25–63; David A. Burney and Ramilisonina, 'The Kilopilopitsofy, Kidoky, and Bokyboky: Accounts of Strange Animals from Belo-sur-mer, Madagascar, and the Megafaunal "Extinction Window"', *American Anthropologist*, c/4 (1998), pp. 957–66.

21 Edgar Williams, *Ostrich* (London, 2012), p. 284.

22 Laurie R. Godfrey and William L. Jungers, 'The Extinct Sloth Lemurs of Madagascar', *Evolutionary Anthropology*, xii/6 (2003), pp. 252–63.

23 Burney and Ramilisonina, 'The Kilopilopitsofy'.

24 Paul P. A. Mazza, 'If Hippopotamuses Cannot Swim, How Did They Colonize Islands?', *Lethaia*, xlvii/4 (2014), pp. 494–9.

25 Robert A. McCall, 'Implications of Recent Geological Investigations of the Mozambique Channel for the Mammalian Colonization of Madagascar', *Proceedings of the Royal Society of London B*, cclxiv/1382 (1997), pp. 663–5.

2 MUD, MUD, GLORIOUS MUD

1 S. K. Eltringham, *The Hippos, Natural History and Conversation* (London, 1999), p. 184.

2 Holbrook Jackson, *The Complete Nonsense of Edward Lear* (New York, 1951), p. 288.

3 Samuel George Morton, 'Additional Observations on a New Living Species of Hippopotamus of Western Africa (*Hippopotamus liberiensis*)', *Journal of the Academy of the Natural Sciences of Philadelphia*, i (1849), pp. 3–14.

4 P. T. Robinson, 'River Horses and Water Cows', in *The Pepper Bird* (San Diego, ca, 1996), pp. 5–6.

5 Eltringham, *The Hippos*, p. 184.

6 'Pygmy Hippopotamus *Choeropsis liberiensis* (Morton 1849)', International Studbook 2012, Basel Zoo, Switzerland, p. 149.

7 Gabriella L. Flacke et al., 'The Pygmy Hippopotamus *Choeropsis liberiensis* (Morton, 1844): Bringing to Light Research Priorities for the Largely Forgotten, Smaller Hippo Species', *Der Zoologische Garten*, LXXXIV/5 (2015), pp. 234–65.

8 Michael Locke, 'Structure of Ivory', *Journal of Morphology*, CCLXIX/4 (2008), pp. 423–50.

9 Eltringham, *The Hippos*, p. 184.

10 Robert Twigger, *Red Nile: A Biography of the World's Greatest River* (London, 2014), p. 466.

11 Karen Paolillo, *A Hippo Love Story* (London, 2014), p. 219.

12 William E. Barklow, 'Amphibious Communication with Sound in Hippos, *Hippopotamus amphibious*', *Animal Behaviour*, LXVIII/5 (2004), pp. 1125–32.

13 M. J. Orliac, F. Guy and R. Lebrun, 'Osteological Connections of the Pesterol Bone of the Extant Hippopotamidae *Hippopotamus amphibious* and *Choeropsis liberiensis*', *MorphoMuseum*, I/1 (2014), pp. 1–6.

14 Maria Maust-Mohl, Joseph Soltis and Diana Reiss, 'Acoustic and Behavioural Repertoires of the Hippopotamus (*Hippopotamus amphibius*)', *Journal of the Acoustical Society of America*, CXXXVIII/2 (2015), p. 545.

15 Brittany L. Coughlin and Frank E. Fish, 'Hippopotamus Underwater Locomotion: Reduced-gravity Movements for a Massive Mammal', *Journal of Mammology*, XC/3 (2009), pp. 675–9; M. Hilderbrand, 'The Quadrupedal Gaits of Vertebrates: The Timing of Leg Movements Relates to Balance, Body Shape, Agility, Speed, and Energy Expenditure', *Bioscience*, XXXIX (1989), pp. 766–75.

16 W. P. Wall, 'The Correlation Between High Limb-bone Density and Aquatic Habits in Recent Mammals', *Journal of Paleontology*, LVII/2 (1983), pp. 197–207.

17 Coughlin and Fish, 'Hippopotamus Underwater Locomotion'.

18 Frank Buckland, 'The Hippopotamus and Her Baby', *Popular Science Monthly*, III (1873), pp. 85–90.

19 R. G. Ruggiero, 'Interspecific Feeding Association: Mutualism and Semi-parasitism Between Hippopotami *Hippopotamus amphibious* and African Jacanas *Actophilornis africanus*', *Ibis*, CXXXVIII/2 (1996), pp. 346–8.

20 Paolillo, *A Hippo Love Story*, p. 219.

21 Eltringham, *The Hippos*, p. 184.

22 Liora Kolska Horwitz and Eitan Tchernov, 'Cultural and Environmental Implications of Hippopotamus Bone Remains in Archaeological Contexts in the Levant', *Bulletin of the American Schools of Oriental Research*, CCLXXX (1990), pp. 67–76.

23 Charles F. Partington, 'Hippopotamus', in *The British Cyclopaedia of Natural History*, vol. II (London, 1836), pp. 749–54.

24 Yoko Saikawa et al., 'Pigment Chemistry: The Red Sweat of the Hippopotamus', *Nature*, CCCCXXIX/363 (2004), p. 363; Kimiko Hashimoto, Yoko Saikawa and Masaya Nakata, 'Studies on the Red Sweat of the *Hippopotamus amphibious*', *Pure and Applied Chemistry*, LXXIX/4 (2007), pp. 507–17.

25 Yoko Saikawka et al., 'Synthesis of Hipposudoric Acid and Norhipposudoric Acids: The Pigments Responsible for the Color Reaction of the Red Sweat of *Hippopotamus amphibious*', *Tetrahedron Letters*, XLVII/15 (2006), pp. 2535–8.

26 Flacke et al., 'The Pygmy Hippopotamus'.

27 Eltringham, *The Hippos*, p. 184.

28 Leejiah Jonathan Dorward, 'New Record of Cannibalism in the Common Hippo', *Hippopotamus amphibius* (Linnaeus 1758)', *African Journal of Ecology*, LIII/3 (2015), pp. 385–7.

29 Ibid.

30 Richard J. T. Verweij et al., 'Grazing Lawns Contribute to the Subsistence of Mesoherbivores on Dystrophic Savannas', *Oikos*, CXIV/1 (2006), pp. 108–16.

31 Douglas J. McCauley et al., 'Carbon Stable Isotopes Suggest the Hippopotamus-vectored Nutrients Subsidize Aquatic Consumers in an East African River', *Ecosphere*, VI/4 (2015), pp. 1–11; Aenne Post, *The Hippopotamus: Nothing but a Nuisance?*, PhD thesis (University of Amsterdam, 1997), pp. 87–117 (p. 109).

32 T. S. McCarthy, W. N. Ellery and A. Bloem, 'Some Observations on the Geomorphological Impact of Hippopotamus (*Hippopotamus amphibius L.*) in the Okavango Delta, Botswana', *African Journal of Ecology*, XXXVI/1 (1998), pp. 44–56.

33 Richard Dispard Estes, Chapter Thirteen, in *The Behaviour Guide to African Mammals* (Los Angeles, CA, 1991), pp. 222–6; Richard D. Estes, Chapter Seventeen, in *The Safari Companion: A Guide to Watching African Mammals* (Harare, Zimbabwe, 1999), pp. 185–9.

34 Hilderbrand, 'The Quadrupedal Gaits of Vertebrates'.

35 R. M. Laws and G. Clough, 'Observations on Reproduction in the Hippopotamus *Hippopotamus amphibius Linn*', *Symposium Zoological Society of London*, XV (1966), pp. 117–40.

36 Eltringham, *The Hippos*, p. 184.

37 Jan Pluháček and Beatrice L. Steck, 'Different Sex Allocations in Two Related Species: The Case of the Extant Hippopotamus', *Ethology*, CXXI/5 (2015), pp. 462–71.

38 Flacke et al., 'The Pygmy Hippopotamus'.

39 Ibid.

40 Ibid.

41 Rowen B. Martin, 'Hippopotamus', *Transboundary Species Project, Ministry of Environment and Tourism, Namibia* (2005), p. 74.

42 Ibid.

43 Ibid.

44 Eltringham, *The Hippos*, p. 184.

45 Martin, 'Hippopotamus', p. 74.

3 WATER HORSE

1 J. Desmond Clark et al., 'Stratigraphic, Chronological and Behavioural Contexts of Pleistocene *Homo sapiens* from Middle Awash, Ethiopia', *Nature*, CDXXIII (2003), pp. 747–52.

2 Ibid.

3 David Coulson and Alec Campbell, 'Rock Art of the Tassili n'Ajjer, Algeria', *Trust for African Rock Art, Kenya, Africa* (2010), pp. 24–38.

4 Victoria Waldock, 'The Taleschout Hippos: An Enigmatic Site in the Messak Settafet, Southwest Libya', *Sahara*, XXI (2010) pp. 93–106.
5 Alec Campbell and David Coulson, 'Big Hippo Site, Oued Afar, Algeria', *Sahara*, XXI (2010), pp. 81–92.
6 T. Säve-Söderbergh, *On Egyptian Representations of Hippopotamus Hunting as a Religious Motive* (Uppsala, 1953), p. 60.
7 Ibid.
8 José Lull and Juan Antonio Belmonte, 'The Constellations of Ancient Egypt', Chapter Six, in *In Search of Cosmic Order: Selected Essays on Egyptian Archaeoastronomy*, ed. J. A. Belmonte and M. Shaltout (Cairo, 2009), pp. 57–194.
9 'The Hippopotamus', *Notes and Queries* (15 June 1850), pp. 35–6.
10 Glen J. Kuban, 'Does the Bible Describe Dinosaurs in Job 40 and 41?', Paluxy Dinosaur/'Man Track' Controversy (2008), http://paleo.cc/paluxy/behemoth.htm, accessed 18 March 2016.
11 Raymond Crawford, 'Legends and Lore of the Healing Art II', *Lotus Magazine*, X (1919), pp. 25–30.
12 Cassius Dio, Epitome of Book LXXII, *Roman History*; Elliot Kidd, *'Beast Hunts' in Roman Amphitheatres: The Impact of the Venationes on Animal Populations in the Ancient Roman World*, ed. James Duban (Denton, TX, 2012), p. 21.
13 Helen Whitehouse, 'Shipwreck on the Nile: A Greek Novel on a "Lost" Roman Mosaic', *American Journal of Archaeology*, LXXXIX/1 (1985), pp. 129–34.
14 George William Lemon, *English Etymology* (London, 1783).
15 Larry Swanson, *Neuroanatomical Terminology: A Lexicon of Classical Origins and Historical Foundations* (Oxford, 2014), p. 1080.
16 Richard Girling, *The Hunt for the Golden Mole* (London, 2014), p. 312.
17 Georges-Louis Leclerc, Comte de Buffon, 'The Hippopotamus', in *The Natural History of Quadrupeds*, vol. II (Edinburgh, 1830), pp. 321–40.
18 Graham Renshaw, *Natural History Essays* (London, 1904), pp. 114–25; Dirk Albert Hooijer, 'Fact and Fiction in Hippopotamology

(Sampling the History of Scientific Error)', *Osiris*, x (1952), pp. 109–16.

19 Sachiko Kusukawa, 'The *Historia Piscium* (1686)', *Notes and Records of the Royal Society of London*, LIV/2 (2000), pp. 179–97.

20 Rowen B. Martin, 'Hippopotamus', *Transboundary Species Project, Ministry of Environment and Tourism, Namibia* (2005), p. 74; G. C. Shortridge, *The Mammals of South West Africa*, vol. II (London, 1934), p. 648.

21 Frank Buckland, 'The Hippopotamus and Her Baby', *Popular Science Monthly*, III (1873), pp. 85–90.

22 Donald McRea, *Every Second Counts: The Race to Transplant the First Human Heart* (London, 2007), p. 16.

23 Girling, *The Hunt for the Golden Mole*, p. 312; G. Cuvier, *Annales du muséum national d'histoire naturelle de Paris*, V (1804), pp. 99–112.

24 Cuvier, *Annales*; 'The Hippopotamus', *New York Dental Journal*, ed. W. B. Roberts and Frank H. Norton (New York, 1861), pp. 244–52.

25 F. N. Egerton, 'A History of the Ecological Sciences, Part 24: Buffon and Environmental Influences on Animals', *Bulletin of the Ecological Society of America*, LXXXVIII/2 (2007), pp. 146–59.

26 Charles F. Partington, 'Hippopotamus', in *The British Cyclopaedia of Natural History*, vol. II (1836), pp. 749–54.

4 THE ILLUSTRIOUS STRANGER

1 T. Säve-Söderbergh, *On Egyptian Representations of Hippopotamus Hunting as a Religious Motive* (Uppsala, 1953), p. 60.

2 Ibid.

3 Jennie Cohen, 'Did a Hippo Kill King Tut?', available at www. history.com, accessed 8 March 2017.

4 N. Fawcett and J. C. Zietsman, 'Uluburun: The Discovery and Excavation of the World's Oldest Known Shipwreck', *Akroterion*, XXXVI (2001), pp. 5–20.

5 Ibid.

6 Father Gavazzi, 'Relics and Images', *New York Times* (4 May 1853).

7 Michael Locke, 'Structure of Ivory', *Journal of Morphology*, CCLXIX/4 (2008), pp. 423–50.

8 Charles F. Partington, 'Hippopotamus', in *The British Cyclopaedia of Natural History*, vol. II (1836), pp. 749–54.

9 Robert L. Engelmeier, 'The History and Development of Posterior Denture Teeth – Introduction, Part I', *Journal of Prosthodontics*, XII/3 (2003), pp. 219–26.

10 'The Hippopotamus', *New York Dental Journal*, ed. W. B. Roberts and Frank H. Norton (1861), pp. 244–52.

11 Robert L. Engelmeier, 'The History and Development of Posterior Denture Teeth – Introduction, Part II: Artificial Tooth Development in America Through the Nineteenth Century', *Journal of Prosthodontics*, XII/4 (2003), pp. 288–301; James Wynbrandt, *The Excruciating History of Dentistry: Toothsome Tales and Oral Oddities from Babylon to Braces* (New York, 1998), pp. 158–62.

12 Mary Dobson, *The Story of Medicine: From Bloodletting to Biotechnology* (London, 2013), p. 110.

13 Partington, 'Hippopotamus'.

14 Ibid.; Robert Twigger, *Red Nile: A Biography of the World's Greatest River* (London, 2014), p. 466.

15 Winston Spencer Churchill, *The River War: An Account of the Reconquest of the Sudan* (London, 1902), p. 502.

16 Twigger, *Red Nile*, p. 466.

17 Ibid.

18 Ibid.

19 Mr and Mrs John Petherick, *Travels in Central Africa, and Explorations of the Western Nile Tributaries* (London, 1869), https://archive.org.

20 Richard Girling, *The Hunt for the Golden Mole* (London, 2014), p. 312.

21 Andrew J. P. Flack, '"The Illustrious Stranger": Hippomania and the Nature of the Exotic', *Anthrozoos*, XXVI (2013), pp. 43–59.

22 'The Hippopotamus', *Illustrated Magazine of Art*, I (1853), pp. 80–82.

23 'The Hippopotamus', *Household Words*, I (1850), pp. 445–9.

24 'Barnum's Museum', *New York Times* (15 August 1861).

25 Ibid.

26 Ibid.

27 A. D. Bartlett, 'The Hippopotamus', in *Wild Animals in Captivity* (London, 1899), pp. 71–85.

28 A. D. Bartlett, *Wild Animals in Captivity* (London, 1899), https://archive.org

29 *New York Times* (September 1883).

30 Bartlett, 'The Hippopotamus'.

31 E. Crisp, 'On Some Points Connected with the Anatomy of the Hippopotamus (*Hippopotamus amphibius*)', *Proceedings of the Zoological Society of London*, XXXIX (1867), pp. 601–12.

32 Jon Mooallem, 'American Hippopotamus', *The Atavist*, XXXII (2013), p. 78.

33 Edgar Williams, *Ostrich* (London, 2013), p. 184.

34 Mooallem, 'American Hippopotamus'.

35 Ibid.

36 Theodore Roosevelt, *African Game Trails: An Account of the African Wanderings of an American Hunter-naturalist* (New York, 1910), p. 583.

37 Hedley A. Chilvers, *Huberta Goes South: A Record of the Lone Trek of the Celebrated Zululand Hippopotamus, 1928–1931* (London, 1932), p. 174.

5 THE GOOD, THE BAD AND THE UGLY

1 Karen Paolillo, *A Hippo Love Story* (Johannesburg, 2014), p. 219.

2 See Daniel Margocsy, 'How One 17th-century Artist Produced a Good Painting of an Animal He'd Never Seen', 12 November 2014, www.slate.com.

3 Lewis Carroll, *Sylvie and Bruno* (London and New York, 1889), p. 88.

4 Bertrand Russell, 'Expanding Mental Universe', *Saturday Evening Post* (18 July 1959).

5 'The Hippopotamus in a New Character', *Punch*, XIX (1850), p. 92.

6 Nina J. Root, 'Victorian England's Hippomania', *Natural History*, CII/2 (1993), pp. 34–9.

7 'A Howl from the Hippopotamus', *Punch*, XXIII (1853), p. 168.

8 Andrew J. P. Flack, '"The Illustrious Stranger": Hippomania and the Nature of the Exotic', *Anthrozoös*, xxvi/7 (2013), pp. 43–59.

9 *Harry and His Hippo*, Cabbage Crunch Dandy Comic Library, no. 35 (Dundee, 1984), p. 66.

10 Advert in Florence Morse Kingsley, *Wings and Fetters: A Story for Girls* (Philadelphia, PA, 1902), p. 302.

11 Peter Young, *Swan* (London, 2008), p. 200.

6 THE MODERN HIPPO

1 Carl Hagenbeck, *Beasts and Men, Being Carl Hagenbeck's Experiences for a Half a Century Among Wild Animals: An Abridged Translation by H.S.R. Elliot and A. G. Thacker* (London, 1912), p. 328.

2 Ibid.

3 Ibid.

4 Graham Renshaw, *Natural History Essays* (London, 1904), pp. 114–25; Graham Renshaw, *More Natural History Essays* (London, 1905), p. 149.

5 William T. Hornaday, 'Our Pygmy Hippopotami', *Zoological Society Bulletin* (New York Zoological Society), xvi/52 (1912), pp. 877–9.

6 Renshaw, *Natural History Essays*; Renshaw, *More Natural History Essays*.

7 Ibid.

8 Hans Schomburgk, 'On the Trail of the Pygmy Hippo: An Account of the Hagenbeck Expedition to Liberia', *Zoological Society Bulletin* (New York Zoological Society), xvi/52 (1912), pp. 880–85.

9 Andrew J. P. Flack, '"The Illustrious Stranger": Hippomania and the Nature of the Exotic', *Anthrozoös*, xxvi/7 (2013), pp. 43–59.

10 'Pygmy Hippopotamus *Choeropsis liberiensis* (Morton 1849)', International Studbook 2012, Basel Zoo, p. 149.

11 'Barnum's Museum', *New York Times* (15 August 1861).

12 William L. Slout, *Clowns and Cannons: The American Circus During the Civil War* (Rockville, MD, 2009), p. 260.

13 Richard J. Reynolds, 'The Ringling-Barnum Hippos 1938–1965', *Bandwagon*, ix/6 (1965), pp. 19–23.

14 Ringling Brothers Route Book (Chicago, IL, 1899).

15 A. D. Bartlett, *Wild Animals in Captivity. Being an Account of the Habits, Food, Management and Treatment of the Beasts and Birds at the Zoo with Reminiscences and Anecdotes* (London, 1899), p. 373.

16 Ibid.

17 Elizabeth Clark, 'Bella and Chaka: The First Hippos at Auckland Zoological Gardens', *The Bartlett Society* (2012), pp. 1–5.

18 Gabriella L. Flacke et al., 'The Pygmy Hippopotamus *Choeropsis liberiensis* (Morton, 1849): Bringing to Light Research Priorities for the Largely Forgotten, Smaller Hippo Species', *Der Zoologische Garten*, LXXXIV/5 (2015), pp. 234–65.

19 Freddy Litten, 'Adieu Hippo: The Nearly Forgotten Victims of the Ueno Zoo During the Second World War', *Zoologische Garten*, LXXXIV (2015), pp. 35–44.

20 William J. Ripple et al., 'Collapse of the World's Largest Herbivores', *Science Advances*, 1/4 (2015), e1400103.

21 Frederick Thurston Drake et al., 'Traumatic Near Amputation Secondary to Hippopotamus Attack: Lessons for Surgeons', *Journal of Surgical Research*, CLXXXVIII/7 (2014), pp. 58–63.

22 David N. Durrheim and Peter A. Leggat, 'Risk to Tourists Posed by Wild Mammals in South Africa', *Journal of Travel Medicine*, VI/3 (1999), pp. 172–9.

23 Christiaan W. Winterbach, Carolyn Whitesell and Michael J. Somers, 'Wildlife Abundance and Diversity as Indicators of Tourism Potential in Northern Botswana', *PLOS One*, X/8 (2015), e0135595.

24 Ibid.; Rowen B. Martin, 'Hippopotamus', in *Transboundary Species Project, Ministry of Environment and Tourism, Namibia* (2005), p. 74.

25 'Conserving the Pygmy Hippo in Sierra Leone', Edge (n.d.), www.edgeofexistence.org, accessed 18 March 2016.

26 April L. Conway et al., 'Local Awareness of Attitudes Towards the Pygmy Hippopotamus *Choeropsis liberiensis* in the Moa River Island Complex Sierra Leone', *Oryx*, XLIX/3 (2015), pp. 550–58.

27 Ben Collen et al., 'Field Surveys for the Endangered Pygmy Hippopotamus *Choeropsis liberiensis* in Sapo National Park, Liberia', *Oryx*, XLV/7 (2011), pp. 35–7.

Select Bibliography

Chilvers, Hedley A., *Huberta Goes South: A Record of the Lone Trek of the Celebrated Zululand Hippopotamus, 1928–1931* (London, 1932)

Eltringham, S. K., *The Hippos: Natural History and Conservation* (London, 1999)

Hagenbeck, Carl, *Beasts and Men, Being Carl Hagenbeck's Experiences for a Half a Century among Wild Animals*, abridged trans. H.S.R Elliot and A. G. Thacker (London, 1912)

McCall Smith, Alexander, *The White Hippo* (London, 1980)

Mooallem, Jon, 'American Hippopotamus', *The Avatist*, XXXII (2013), p. 78

Paolillo, Karen, *A Hippo Love Story* (Johannesburg, 2014)

Roosevelt, Theodore, *African Game Trails: An Account of the African Wanderings of an American Hunter-naturalist* (New York, 1910)

Villalobos, Juan Pablo, *Down the Rabbit Hole* (Barcelona, 2010)

Associations and Websites

AFRICAN WILDLIFE FOUNDATION
www.awf.org/wildlife-conservation/hippopotamus

IUCN RED LIST OF THREATENED SPECIES
www.iucnredlist.org
Provides lots of factual information about both hippo species

HIPPOLOTOFUS – The International Hippo Society, for hippo lovers
and collectors of hippo memorabilia
www.hippos.com/

For interesting everyday facts about the common hippo, visit
HIPPOWORLDS
http://www.hippoworlds.com/

THE PYGMY HIPPO FOUNDATION
http://pygmyhippofoundation.org/pygmy-hippos

THE PYGMY HIPPO STUDBOOK provides lots of information about
captive animals
http://zooreach.org/zoo_WILD_Activities/2013/Bulkmail/
HippoStudbook2012.pdf

SAVE OUR SPECIES
sospecies.org

THE TURGWE HIPPO TRUST, ZIMBABWE, AFRICA
www.savethehippos.info/

ZOOLOGICAL SOCIETY OF LONDON, EDGE OF EXISTENCE
www.edgeofexistence.org

Acknowledgements

Writing this book has been a great pleasure, as the hippopotamus is an animal much loved by those who have written about it, both in ancient and modern times. Most of the sources used in this book are open source and are therefore freely available to anyone with access to the Internet.

I would like to thank my family for their enduring support and for sharing my indulgence in all things hippopotamus. I would like to thank Iain Reid for his interest in the book's progress and his excellent translation into English of papers published originally in German. Finally, I would like to thank the team at Reaktion Books for making this book possible.

Photo Acknowledgements

The author and publishers wish to express their thanks to the below sources of illustrative material and/or permission to reproduce it.

Alamy (Luke Farmer): p. 139; author's collection: pp. 113, 114, 115, 133, 137, 143; Bridgeman Images: p. 140 top (Kremlin Museums); © The British Library Board: p. 100; © The Trustees of the British Museum, London: pp. 60, 61, 63, 70, 73, 77, 79, 96, 101, 109, 120; Dmitry Bogdanov: p. 17; Cloudzilla: p. 159; David Coulson – TARA: p. 59; Deviant Art: pp. 16, 19 (WillemSvdMerwe); Getty Images: pp. 62, 64 bottom, 72 (DEA/G Dagli Orti), 74 (DEA /V. Pirozzi), 89 (DEA Picture Library), 90 (DEA/G Dagli Orti); iStockphoto: pp. 46 (ThePalmer), 66 (JonnyJim), 153 (Whiteway); Library of Congress, Washington, DC: p. 150; Mary Evans Picture Library: pp. 56 (BeBa/Iberfoto), 64 top (Ashmolean Museum), 75; Metropolitan Museum of Art, New York: p. 10; Museum of World Culture, Stockholm: p. 87; photos Sally Hope: p. 9; photos Carol Moen Wing and Jereld Wing: pp. 31, 32, 44, 48, 49, 50, 52, 57, 145, 164, 165, 166; New York Public Library: p. 121; REX Shutterstock: pp. 6 (Travel Library), 13 (Gerard Lacz), 14 (Shane Partridge), 24 (Tony Kyriacou), 26 (Library/UIG), 33 (Tony Heald/NPL), 34 (Robert Harding), 35 (Nancy Fleagle), 36 (FLPA/ ImageBROKER), 37 (Mint Images), 39, 40 (ImageBROKER), 41 (Malcolm Schuyl), 45, 53 (ImageBROKER), 55 (Tony Heald/ NPL), 107 (History Archive), 130, 155 (Everett), 158 (Gillard/ANL), 162 (ImageBROKER), 163 (FLPA); courtesy of Bjorn Okholm Skaarup and Cavalier Galleries: p. 140 bottom (Photo Serge Domingie); Victoria and Albert Museum, London: p. 11 (bequeathed by Kineton Parkes in 1938); Wellcome Library, London:

pp. 29, 59, 71, 78, 80, 82, 84, 92, 93, 96; Zoological Society of London:
pp. 27, 76, 98, 146.

Index